GramGram Plus

1

Author Hyunjeong, Kim | **Consultant** Prof. Eunyoung, Park

Editorial Supervisor LLS English Research Center

J PLUS
Language Publishing Co.

Have Fun and Enjoy
the
GRAM GRAM PLUS Series

Welcome to the GRAM GRAM PLUS Series.

This is an introductory grammar series designed to be fun and easy for young learners. It is also designed to promote accurate English speaking and writing skills.

Korean students have traditionally learned English grammar through rote memorization. However, I believe that grammar learning is more effectively realized when instruction is paired with practice. With clear explanations, imaginative illustrations, enjoyable grammar activities and games, the GRAM GRAM PLUS Series allows students to enjoy English grammar as they learn how to use it properly.

The GRAM GRAM PLUS Series provides students with ample opportunities to both practice and improve their English.

Author: Hyunjeong, Kim

Supervisor's Recommendation

Traditionally, many language teachers have taught English grammar according to the Grammar Translation Method. In grammar-translation classes, students learn grammatical rules and then apply those rules by translating sentences between the target language and their native language. Advanced students may be required to translate whole texts word-for-word. However, at the height of the Communicative Approach to language learning in the 1980s and early 1990s, it became fashionable in some quarters to deride so-called "old-fashioned" methods and, in particular, something broadly labeled "Grammar Translation". Nevertheless, we can't ignore grammar in language teaching and learning. In that sense, this series can help both teachers and students by presenting grammar in a communicative way, which can be a very fascinating way to learn English grammar. With a lot of pictures, cartoons, games, and activities, children will be able to 'acquire' English grammar, not 'study' grammar. I hope that many kids will enjoy this joyful process!

Consultant: Prof. Eunyoung, Park

(Ph. D. in English Education / Professor at Methodist Theological University)

GRAM GRAM
PLUS BOOK 1

Unit	Title	Grammar		Topic/Theme	Vocabulary	문법포인트
1	Around Us	Nouns & Pronouns	- Types Of Nouns People, Things, Animals	People & Places Things & Animals	- student, teacher, boy, girl, school, park, playground, dog, bird, tree, desk	사람 · 물건 · 장소 · 동물의 이름
2	Things In The House		- Singular & Plural Nouns -a(n) / -s / -es	Things In The House	- book, watch, umbrella, picture, door, table, chair, dish, cup, apple, fork, egg	한 개 · 여러 개를 나타내는 명사의 형태
3	My Family		- Personal Pronouns 1 I, You, He, She, It	Family	- grandfather, grandmother, father, mother, aunt, uncle, brother, sister, cousin, puppy	나 · 너 · 그 · 그녀 · 그것 (인칭대명사)
4	Happy Family		- Personal Pronouns 2 We, You, They	Family Relations	- grandparents, parents, wife, husband, son, daughter	우리 · 너희 · 그들 (인칭대명사)
5	Neighbors	Be Verb	- Be Verbs In The Affirmative Pronoun + Be Verbs (am, are, is)	People Around Us	- baker, driver, painter, police officer, firefighter, street cleaner, nurse, hair dresser	Be동사 긍정문
6	Jobs		- Be Verbs In The Negative Pronoun + Be Verbs (am, are, is) + Not	Jobs	- doctor, cook, singer, dancer, farmer, pilot, scientist, designer	Be동사 부정문
7	Our Classroom		- Questions With Be Verbs	Classroom Objects	- blackboard, teacher, classmate, class president, desk, scissors, glue, locker, computer	Be동사 의문문
8	Favorite Subjects		- WH-Questions 1 Who ~ ? / What ~ ?	School Subjects	- math, English, art, social studies, P.E., history, science, music	'~은/는 누구니?'에 해당하는 말 (WH-의문사)

Unit	Title	Grammar		Topic/Theme	Vocabulary	문법포인트
9	I Am Tall	Adjectives	- Be Verbs + Adjectives Of Appearance	Appearance	- tall, short, fat, thin, pretty, ugly, young, old, strong, weak	Be동사+외모를 나타내는 형용사
10	Jake Is Angry		- Be Verbs + Adjectives Of Feelings	Feelings	- happy, sad, angry, excited, surprised, jealous, hungry, full	Be동사+감정을 나타내는 형용사
11	It Is A Red Balloon		- Be Verbs + Adjectives Of Color & Size	Colors & Size	- red, yellow, orange, green, blue, white - big, small, long, short	Be동사+색깔, 크기를 나타내는 형용사
12	This Is My Hat		- Possessive Adjectives my, your, his, her, their	Clothes	- pants, jeans, sweater, jacket, blouse, coat, shoes, socks, hat, skirt	'~의'에 해당하는 말(소유격)
13	That Is A Pear	Demonstrative Pronouns	- Demonstrative Pronouns (Singular) this, that	Fruit	- strawberry, cherry, kiwi, watermelon, grapes, pear	'이것은~' '저것은~'에 해당하는 말 (지시대명사)
14	These Are Onions		- Demonstrative Pronouns (Plural) these, those	Vegetables	- onion, potato, carrot, cucumber, garlic, tomato, eggplant, pepper	'이것들은~' '저것들은~'에 해당하는 말 (지시대명사)
15	It Is Spring		- Impersonal Pronoun: It	Weather & Seasons	- spring, summer, fall, winter, sunny, rainy, windy, snowy	'계절 · 날씨'를 나타내는 말(비인칭 주어)
16	What Is That?		- WH-Quiestions 2 What is this(that)? What are these(those)?	Kitchen	- bowl, plate, fork, spoon, knife, chopsticks, napkin, pot	'이것은 무엇이니?' '저것들은 무엇이니'에 해당하는 말 (WH-의문사)

STEP 1

PICTURE

해당 유닛의 핵심 주제와 관련된 단어와 어구를 하나의 재미있는 상황으로 설정하여 삽화로 제시하였습니다. 한눈에 보이는 그림을 통해 핵심 단어들을 쉽고 빠르게 파악할 수 있습니다.

GRAM WORDS

위에 제시된 것 중에서 핵심단어를 뽑아 듣고 그림과 연결할 수 있는 액티비티를 제시하였습니다.

Easy to Follow
4 STEP
Lesson Process

STEP 2

GRAM POINT

해당 유닛의 문법 포인트를 간단한 설명과 도표로 제시하였습니다. 문법 체계에 대한 분석 없이 하나의 문법 사항을 하나의 도표로 빠르게 학습할 수 있습니다. 친절한 GRAM의 한국말 설명은 문법 포인트에 대한 빠른 이해를 도와줍니다.

GRAM CHECK-UP

위에서 확인한 문법 포인트를 간단한 확인문제를 통해 확인해 볼 수 있습니다.

STEP 4

FUNNY GRAM

해당 유닛의 문법 포인트와 핵심 단어를 활용한 게임을 제시하였습니다.
다양한 유형의 게임을 통해 해당 유닛의 문법 포인트와 핵심 단어를 마지막으로 정리, 확인할 수 있도록 하였습니다.

GRAM WRITING

해당 유닛의 문법 사항이 포함된 간단한 문장을 제시하고, 기본적으로는 잘못된 부분을 고쳐 다시 써 보는 활동을 제시하여 '문법'이 실제로 '활용'되는 예를 직접 확인해 볼 수 있도록 하였습니다.

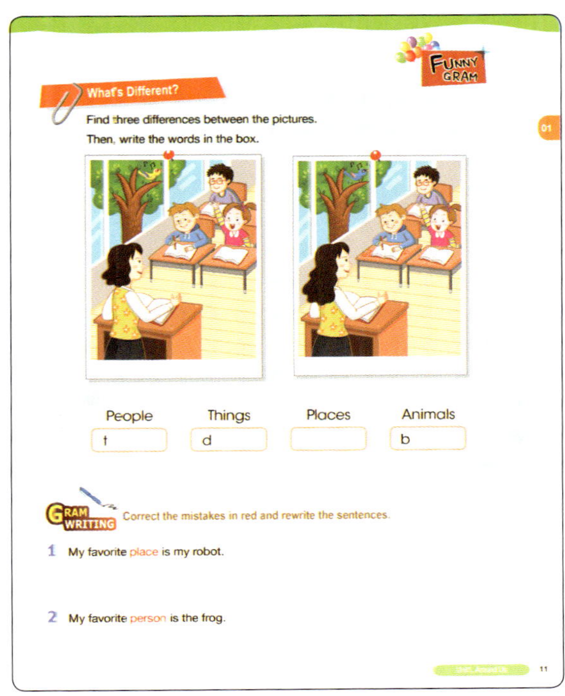

STEP 3

GRAM PRACTICE

해당 유닛의 주제 중심 단어와 문법 포인트를 확인할 수 있는 코너입니다. 알맞은 말 고르기, 단어 완성하기, 빈칸 채우기 등 다양한 형식의 액티비티를 통해 앞서 익힌 단어와 문법 포인트를 쉽고 재미있게 정리해 볼 수 있습니다.

Unit 01

Around Us

Track 1 ☐ Listen ☐ Repeat ☐ Point

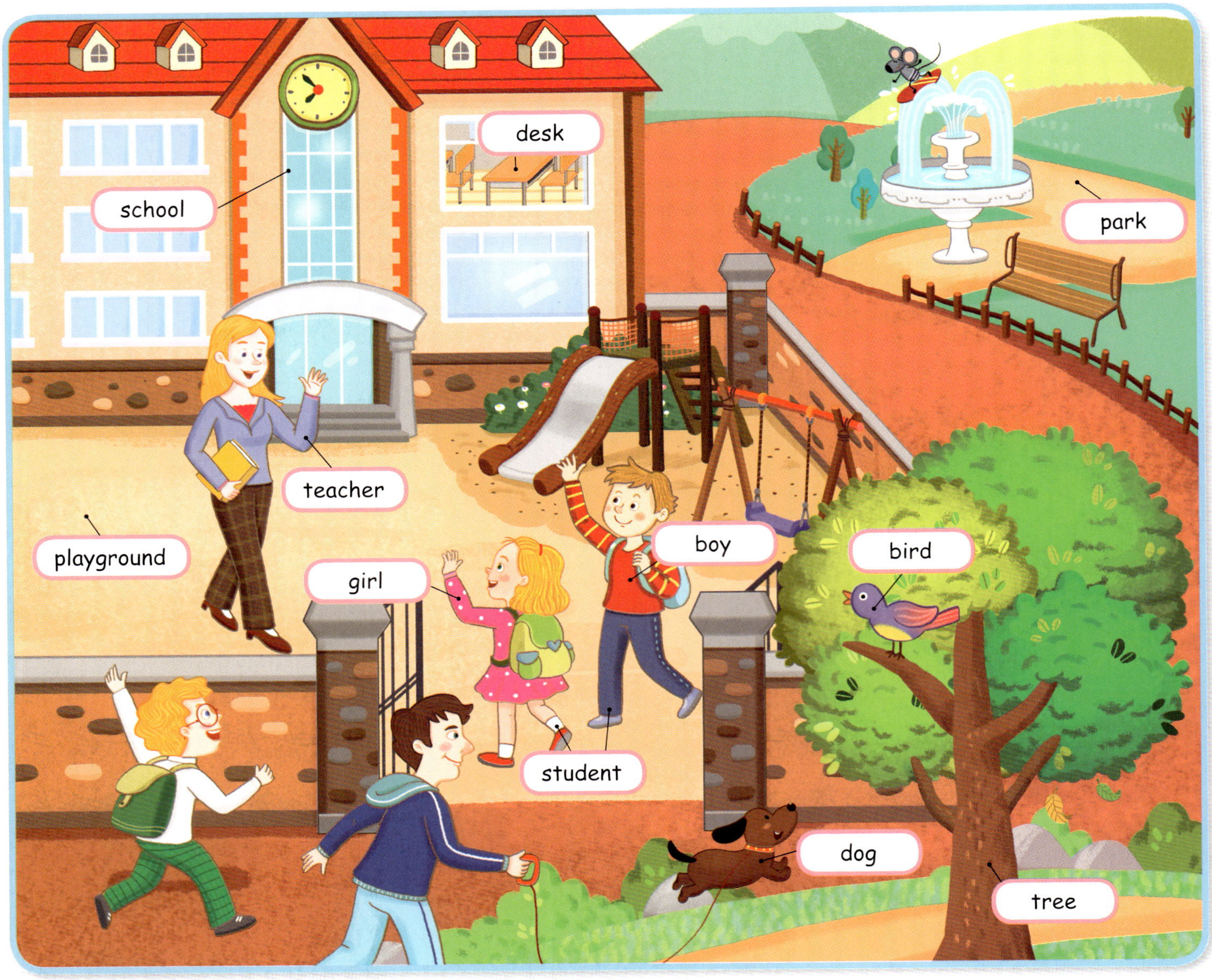

GRAM WORDS Track 2 ABC **Listen and number the pictures in order.** Track 3

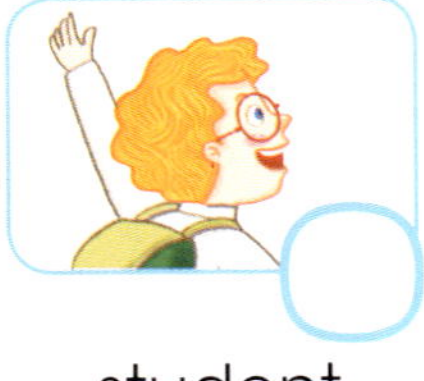

student

teacher

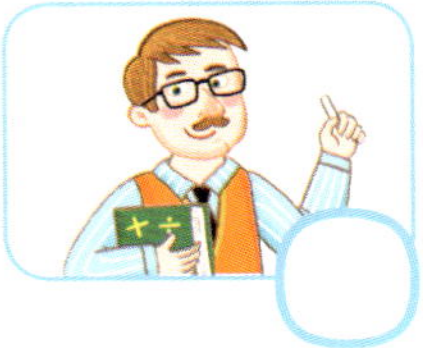

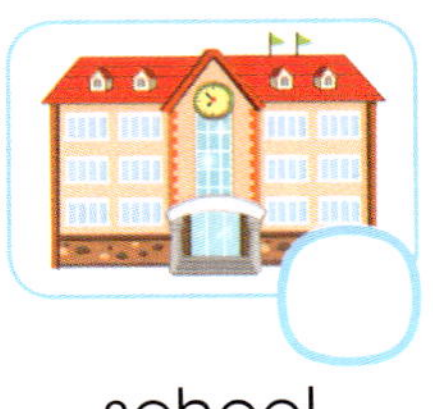

school

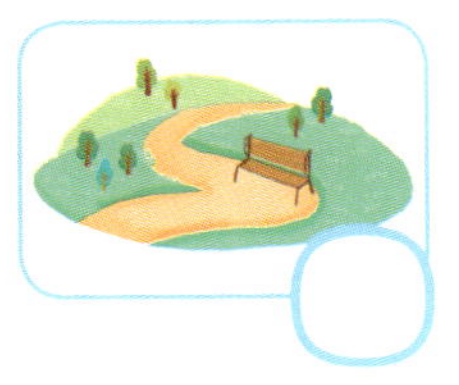

park

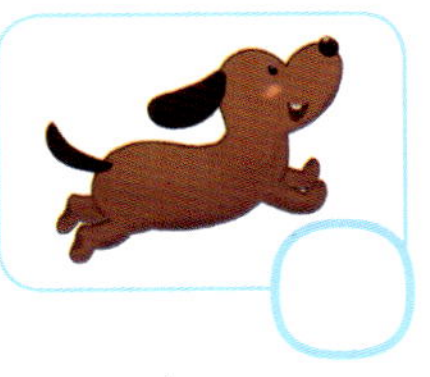

dog

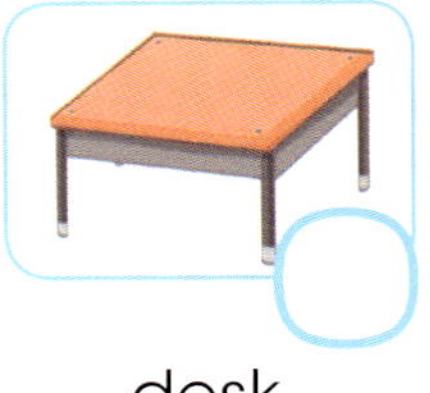

desk

People / Things / Places / Animals

Types of Nouns

People	Things	Places	Animals
teacher	table	school	dog

Examples

- People: boy / girl / student / teacher
- Things: tree / desk / pen / orange
- Places: park / school / house / playground
- Animals: dog / cat / bird / frog

G RAM CHECK UP

Look and write the correct letters.
(people → PE / things → T / places → PL / animals → A)

1 

boy

2 

park

3 

bird

4 

dog

5 

school

6 

desk

A. Look and circle the pictures.

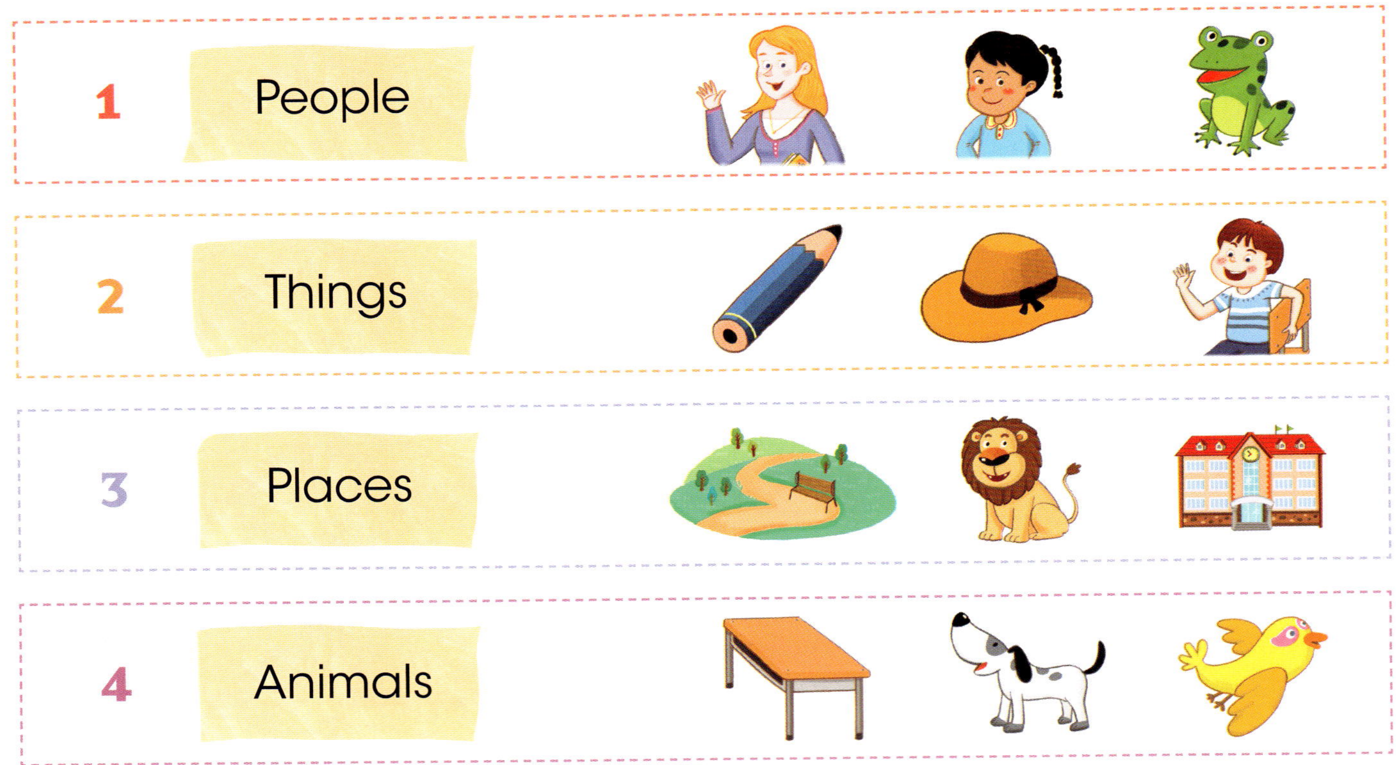

B. Complete the words and match to the correct types.

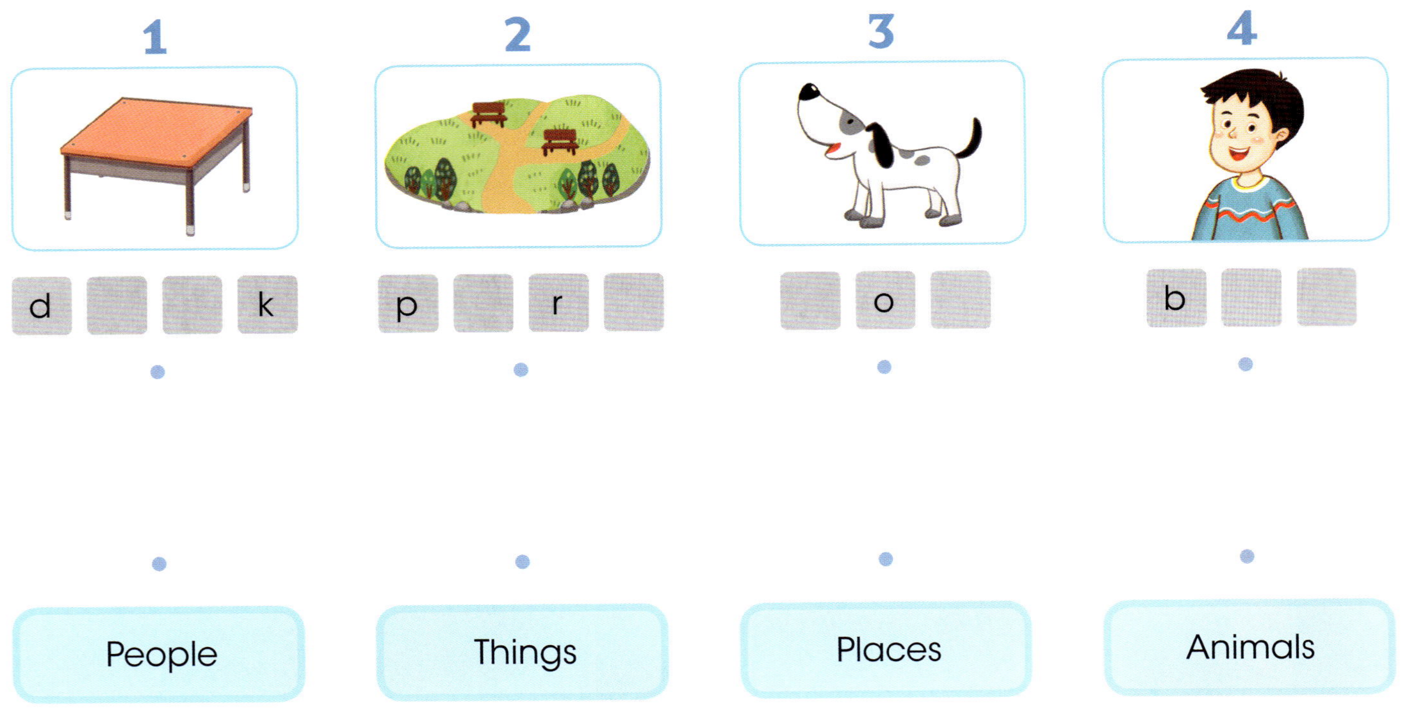

What's Different?

Find three differences between the pictures.

Then, write the words in the box.

People	Things	Places	Animals
t	d		b

GRAM WRITING Correct the mistakes in red and rewrite the sentences.

1 My favorite place is my robot.

____

2 My favorite person is the frog.

____

Things In The House

☐ **Listen**   ☐ **Repeat**   ☐ **Point**

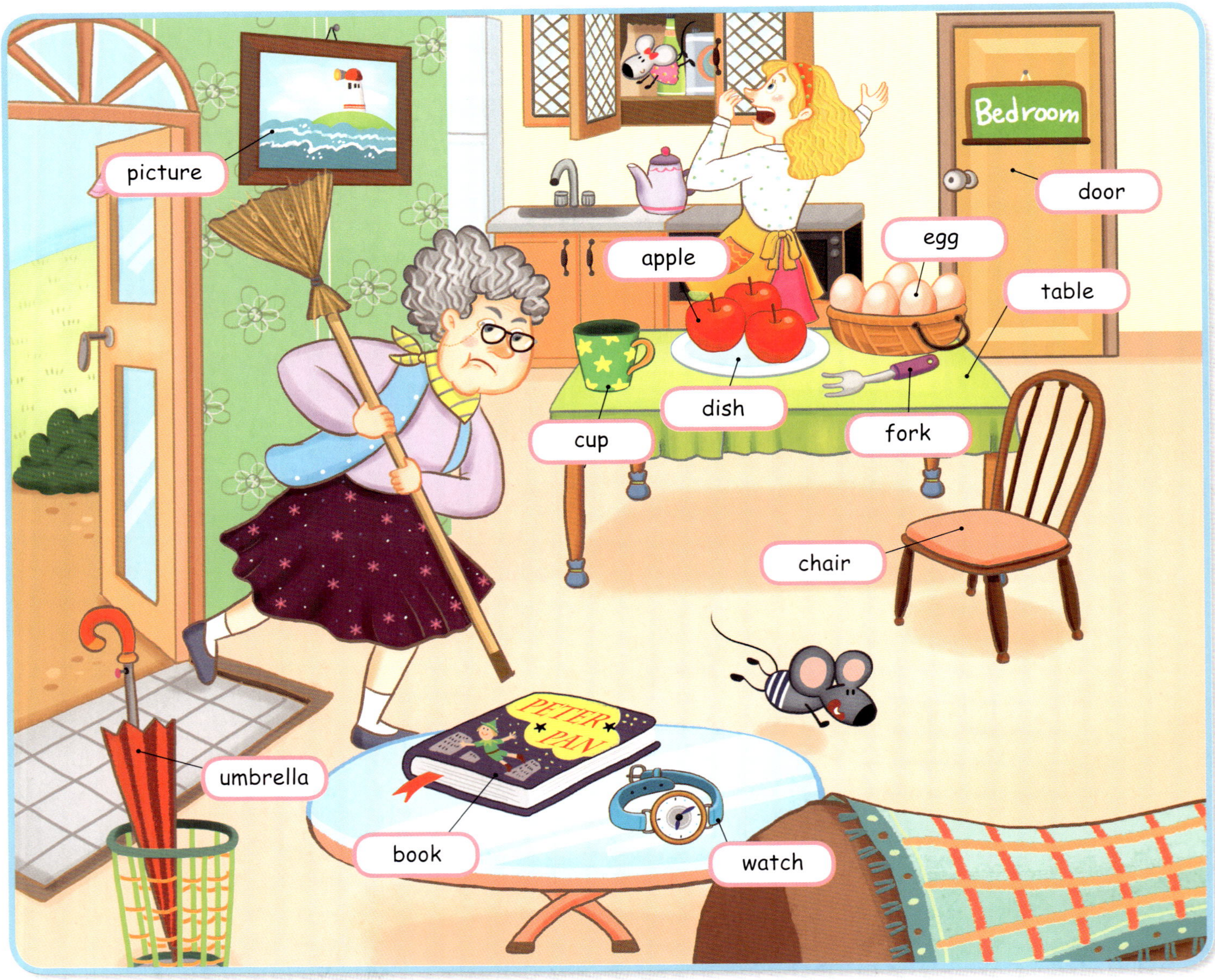

ABC   Listen and number the pictures in order.

a cup	an apple	a dish	a watch	a book	an umbrella

Singular Nouns

- **Consonants:** b c d f g h j k l m n p q r s t v w x y z

  a + consonants: a book / a cup / a dish / a watch

- **Vowels:** a e i o u

  an + vowels: an apple / an egg / an umbrella

Plural Nouns

Noun + -s

a book → books

a cup → cups

an apple → apples

Noun + -es

a dish → dishes

a watch → watches

a bus → buses

GRAM CHECK UP   Look and write O or X.

1 

an book

2 

a cup

3 

an umbrella

4 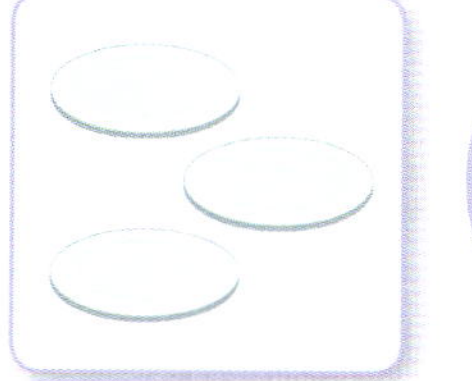

dishes

5 

watchs

6 

apples

GRAM PRACTICE

A. Look and write the correct word.

1

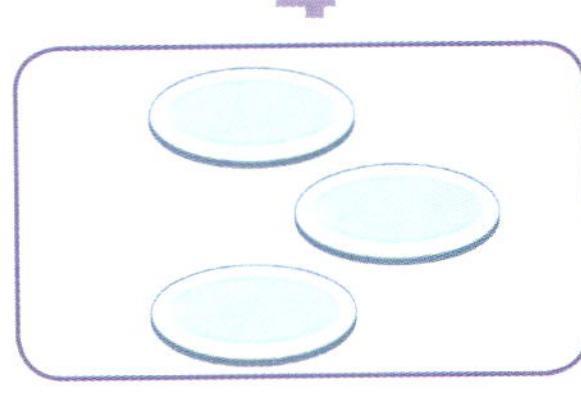

______ book

2

______ umbrella

3

______ cup

4

dish______

5

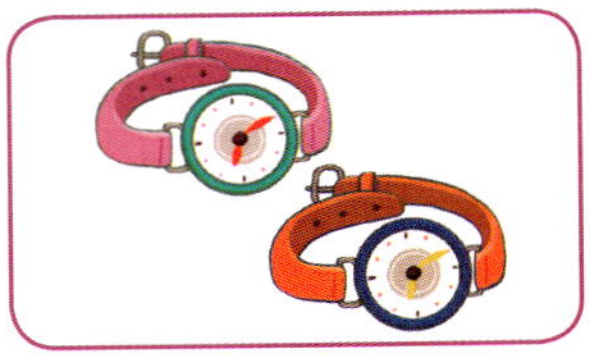

watch______

6

apple______

7

______ egg

8

picture______

9

______ chair

B. Write the correct words in the boxes.

1 a book → three ______

2 an apple → five ______

3 an ______ → two umbrellas

4 an egg → seven ______

5 a dish → three ______

Coin Flick Game

Flick a coin onto the pictures. Convert the singular nouns to plurals of the picture that the coin lands on.

GRAM WRITING Correct the mistakes in red and rewrite the sentences.

1 I have ten egg. I eat two egges.

2 I eat five an apple. Oh, I'm full.

My Family

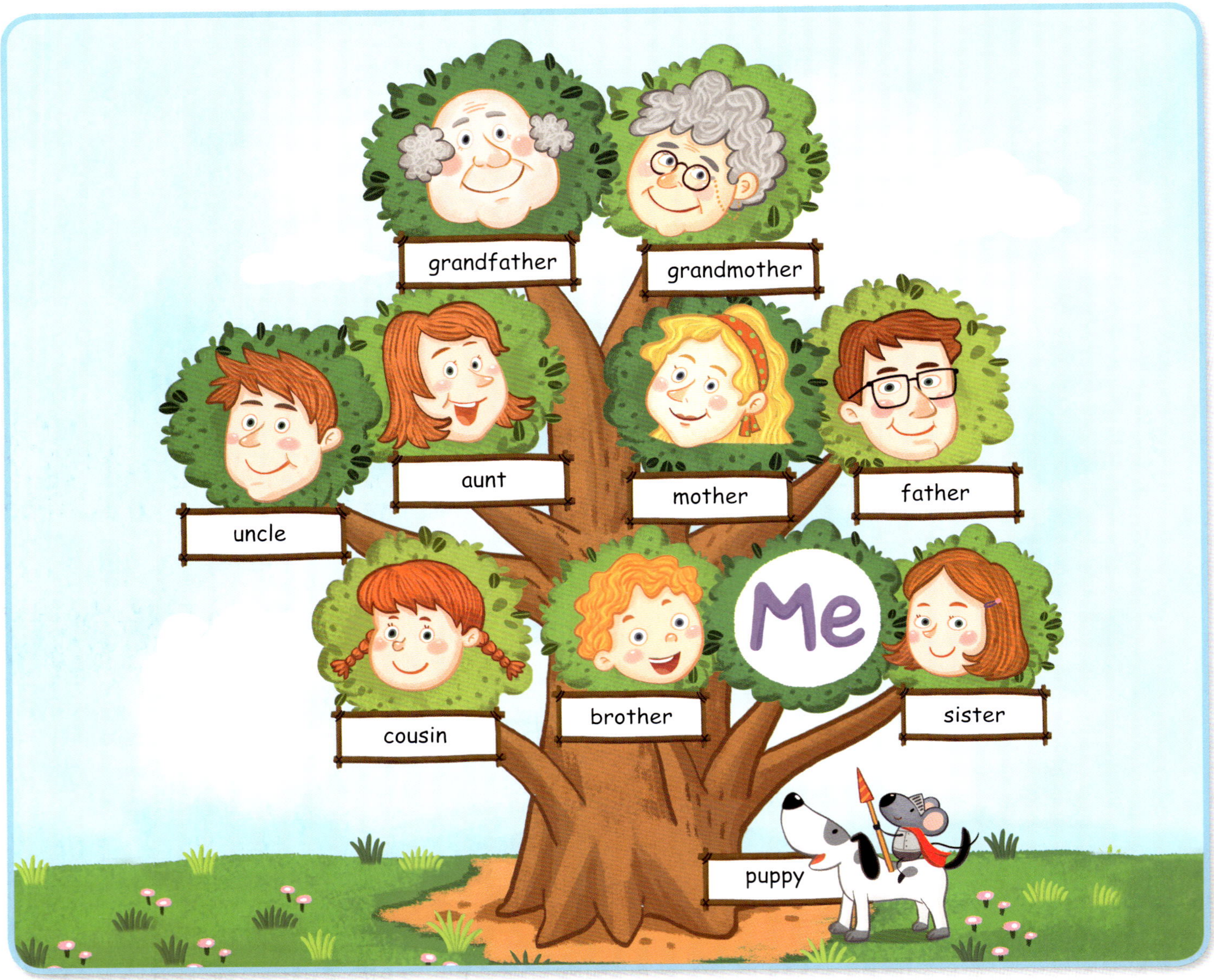

GRAM WORDS Track 8 **ABC** Listen and number the pictures in order.  Track 9

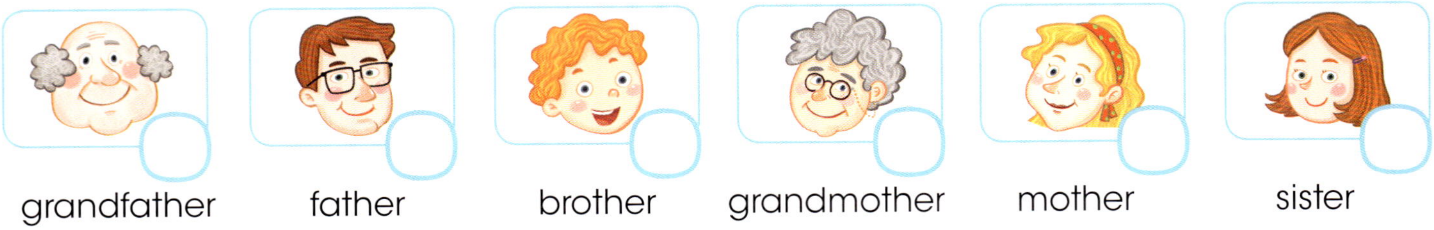

grandfather

father

brother

grandmother

mother

sister

GRAM POINT I / You / He / She / It

Singular Pronouns

People	Animals / Things
I / You / She / He	It

Examples

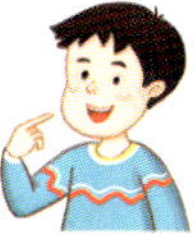

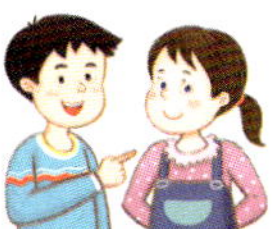

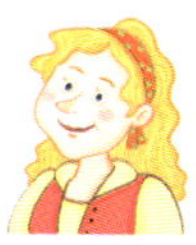

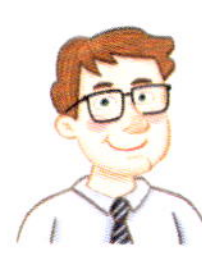

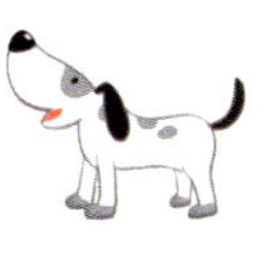

I

You

She

He

It

사람이나 동물 혹은 물건 등을 지칭할 때 쓰는 말을 인칭대명사라고 해!
인칭대명사에는 'I(나)', 'You(너)', 'She(그녀)', 'He(그)', 그리고 'It(그것)'이 있단다. 잘 기억해두자.

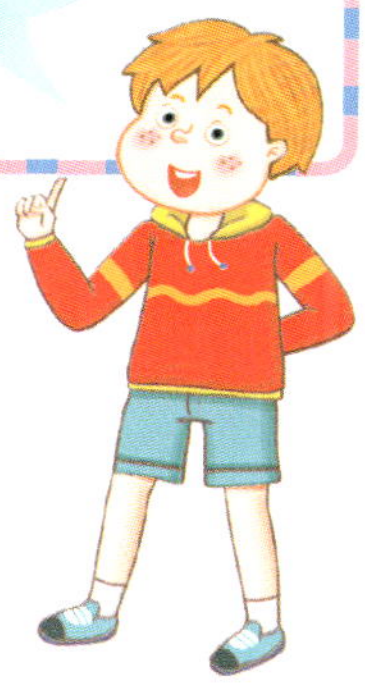

GRAM CHECK UP Look and write O or X.

1 ◯
She

2 ◯
He

3 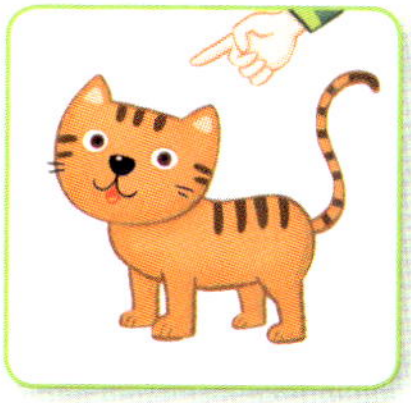 ◯
I

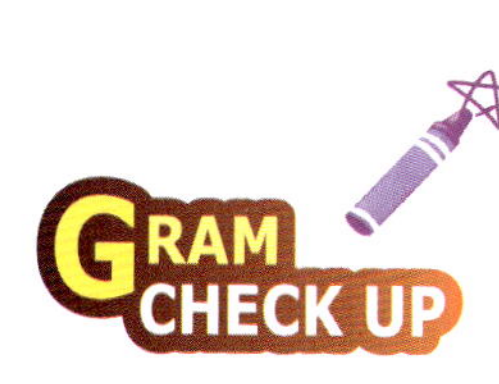

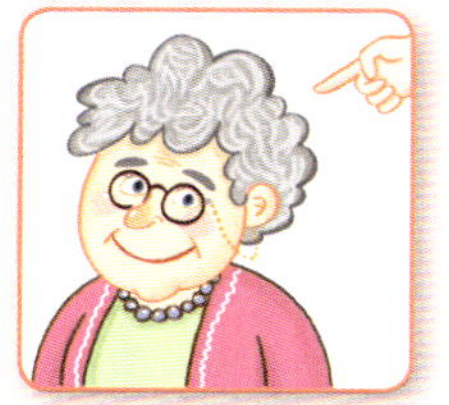

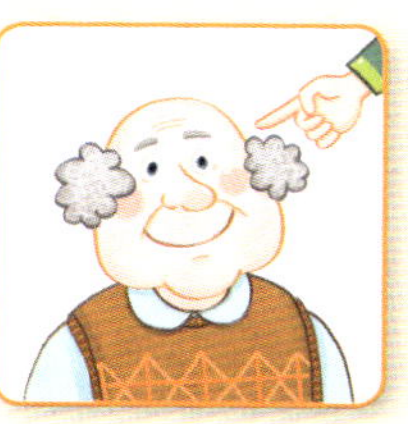

4 ◯
You

5 ◯
He

6 ◯
It

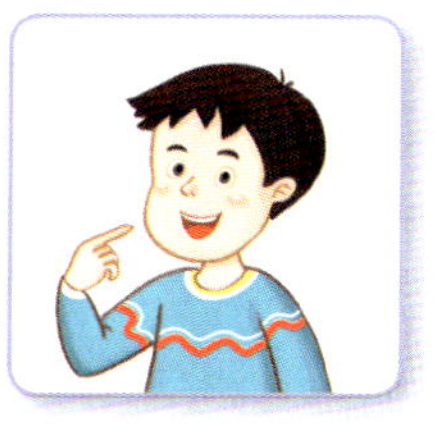

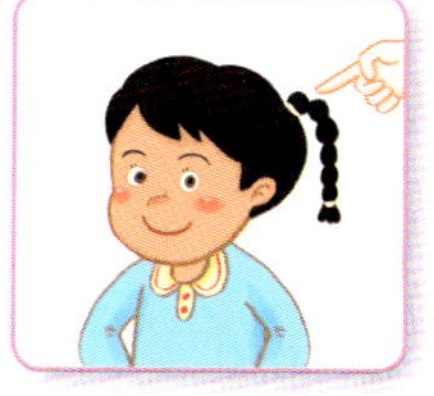

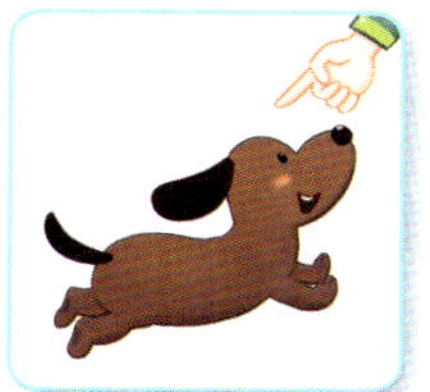

GRAM PRACTICE

A. Write the correct pronoun for each group of words.

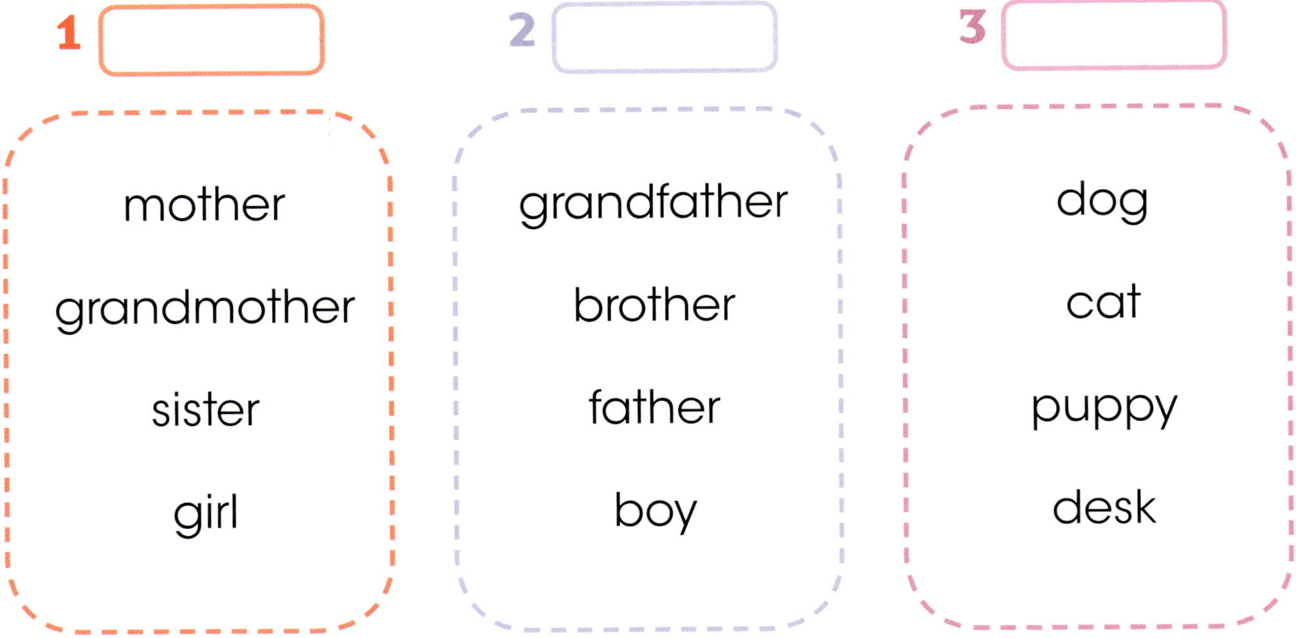

1	2	3
mother	grandfather	dog
grandmother	brother	cat
sister	father	puppy
girl	boy	desk

B. Look and write the correct words from the box.

Word Box: I   He   She   It

1. father _______
2. mother _______
3. brother _______
4. sister _______
5. me _______
6. puppy _______

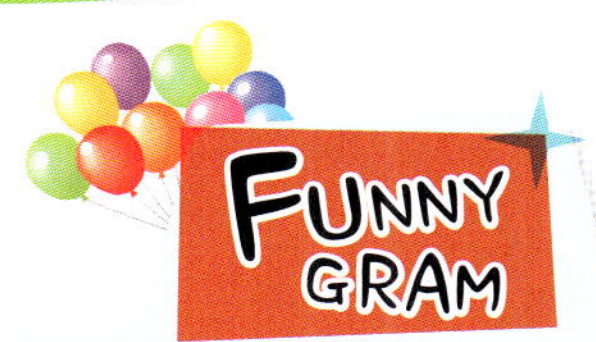

Find The Way

FUNNY GRAM

Help Pinocchio find his way. Then write the singular pronouns in order.

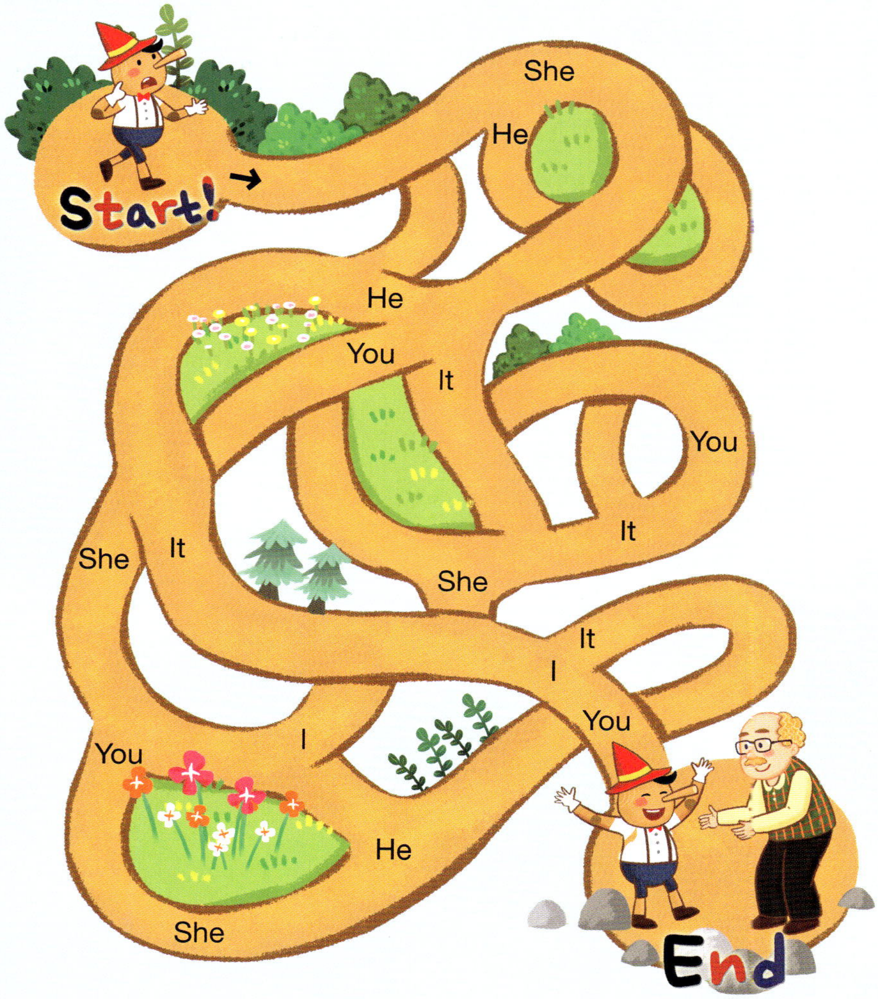

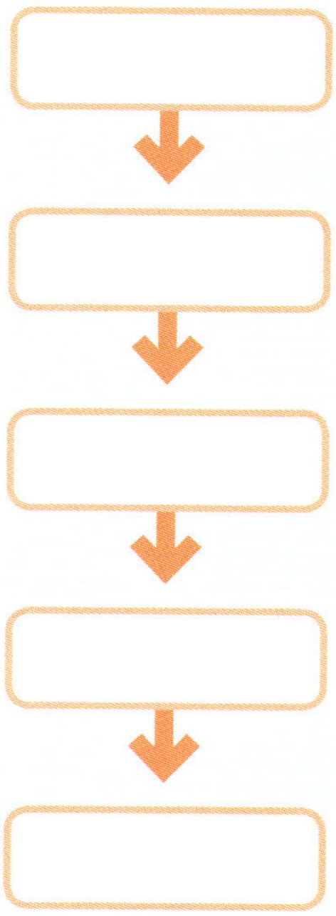

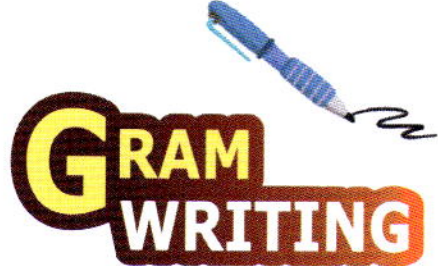

GRAM WRITING

Correct the mistakes in red and rewrite the sentences.

1 He is my mother. It love my mother.

2 She is my grandfather. You is generous.

Happy Family

Unit 04

Track 10 ☐ Listen ☐ Repeat ☐ Point

 **GRAM WORDS** Track 11  Listen and number the pictures in order. Track 12 

grandparents

son

daughter

wife

parents

husband

We / You / They

Plural Pronouns

People	Animals / Things
We / You / They	They

Examples

We You They They

GRAM CHECK UP Look and write O or X.

1 

You

2 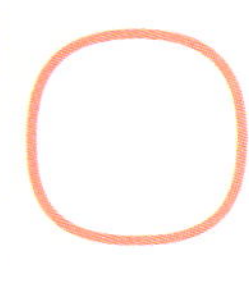

They

3 

We

4 

We

5 

You

6 

They

GRAM PRACTICE

A. Look and write the correct word.

Word Box	We	You	They

1

____

2

____

3

____

4

____

B. Write down *They* or *We*.

1 My parents and I → ________________

2 Two tigers → ________________

3 My grandparents and I → ________________

4 One dog and two cats → ________________

5 A son and his parents → ________________

Family Picture

Draw your family members.

Then stick the correct plural pronouns on the picture.

GRAM WRITING Correct the mistakes in red and rewrite the sentences.

1 I have two sisters. You are kind.

2 My parents are generous. We love me.

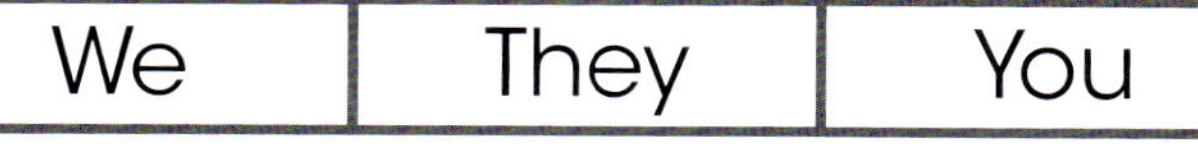

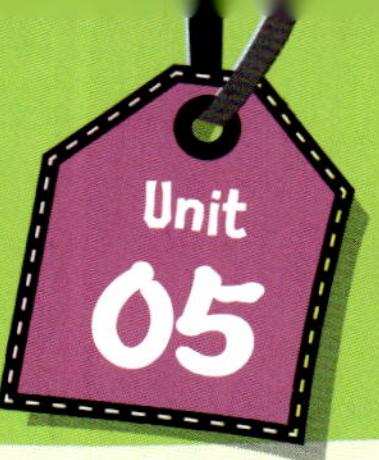

Unit 05 Neighbors

Track 13 □ Listen □ Repeat □ Point

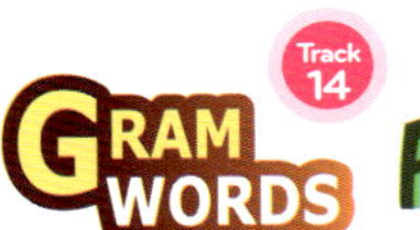

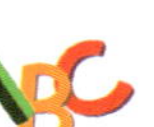

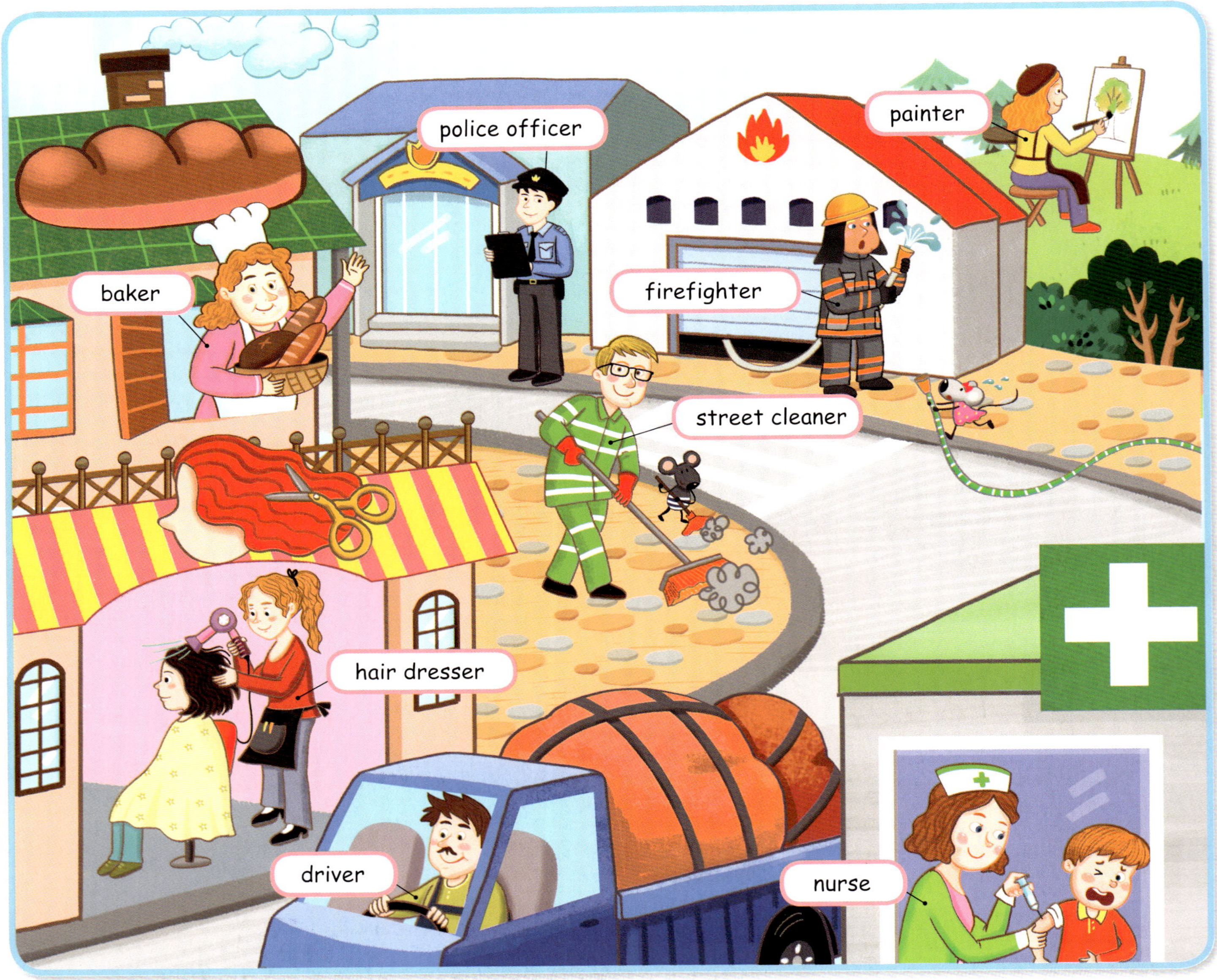

GRAM WORDS ABC Track 14

Listen and number the pictures in order. Track 15

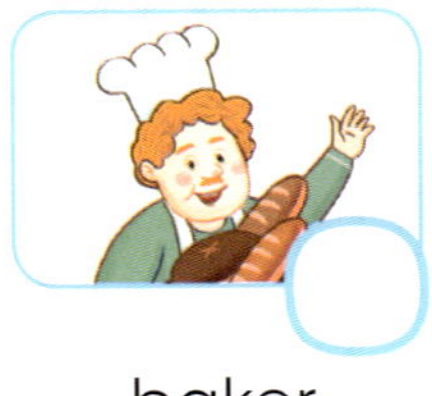

baker

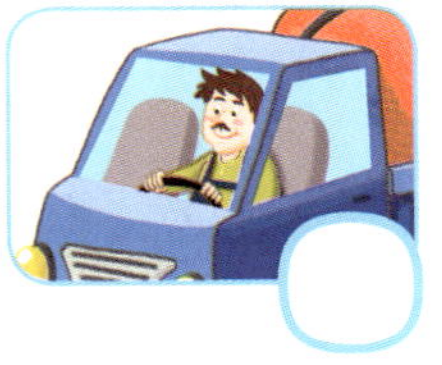

driver

painter

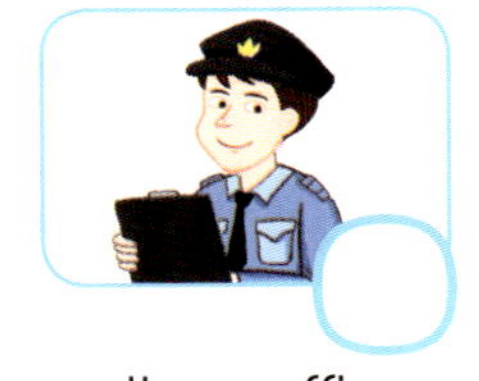

police officer

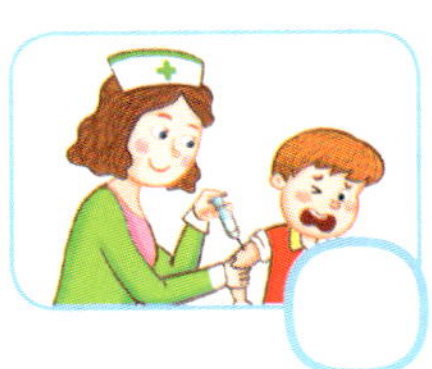

nurse

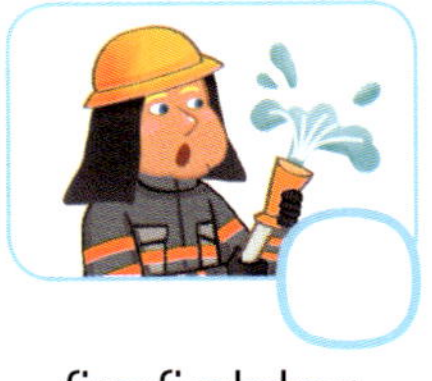

firefighter

Pronoun + Be verb

Singular			Plural		
I	am	I'm	We		We're
You	are	You're	You		You're
He		He's	They	are	
She	is	She's			They're
It		It's	They		

05

Examples

- I am (= I'm) a student.
- He is (= He's) a teacher.
- We are (= We're) students.
- They are (= They're) teachers.

GRAM **CHECK UP**   Look and write O or X.

1 

We is

2 

I am

3 

You are

4 

He is

5 

She am

6 

They is

GRAM PRACTICE

A. Match to the correct Be verbs and short forms.

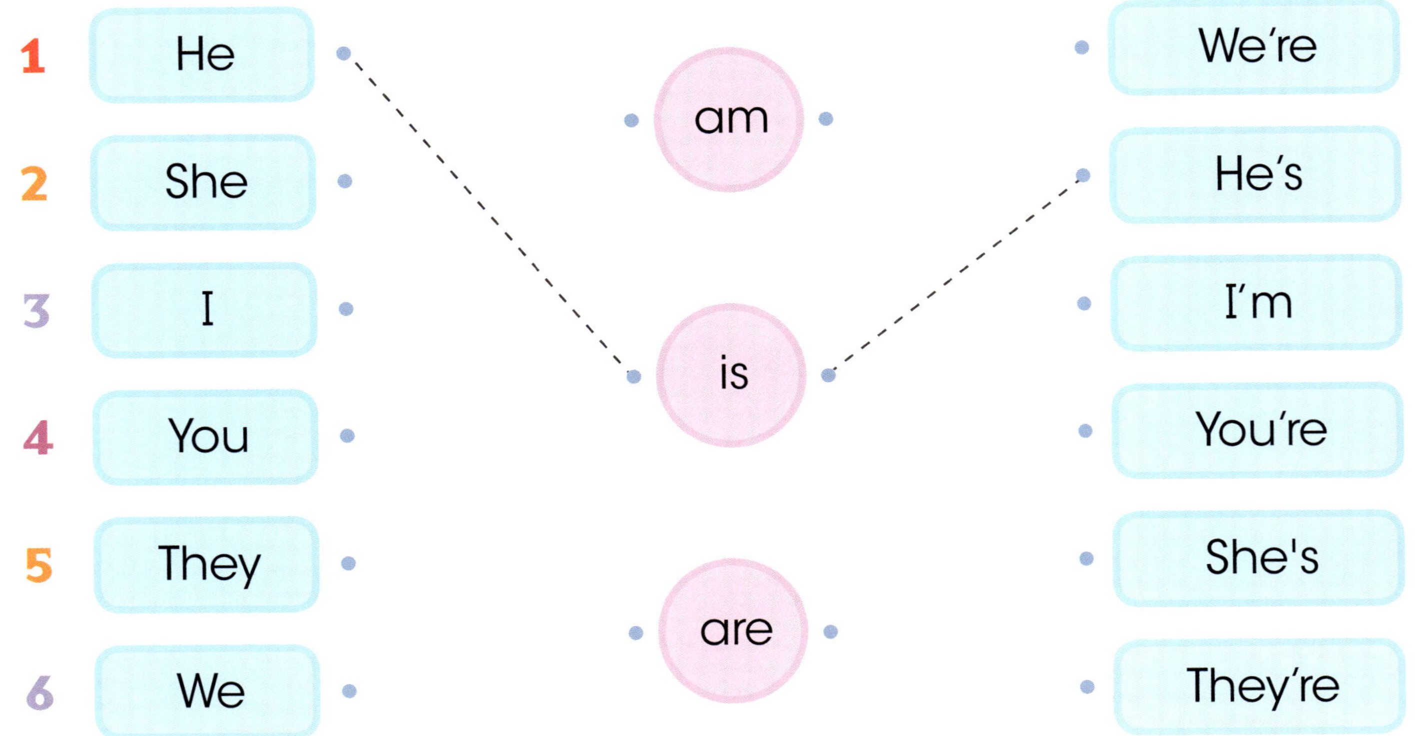

B. Fill in the blanks and trace the words.

1 He is a baker.

2 ____________ is a hair dresser.

3 They ____________ firefighters.

4 She ____________ a nurse.

5 ____________ is a painter.

FUNNY GRAM

Pronoun Spinner

Use a pencil and a paper clip. Spin the paper clip. Then say the sentence. (Example: ***"I am a baker."***)

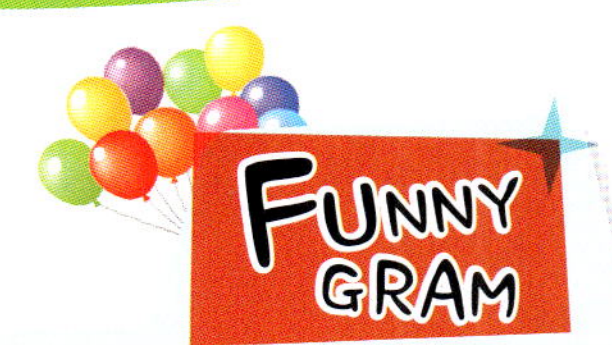

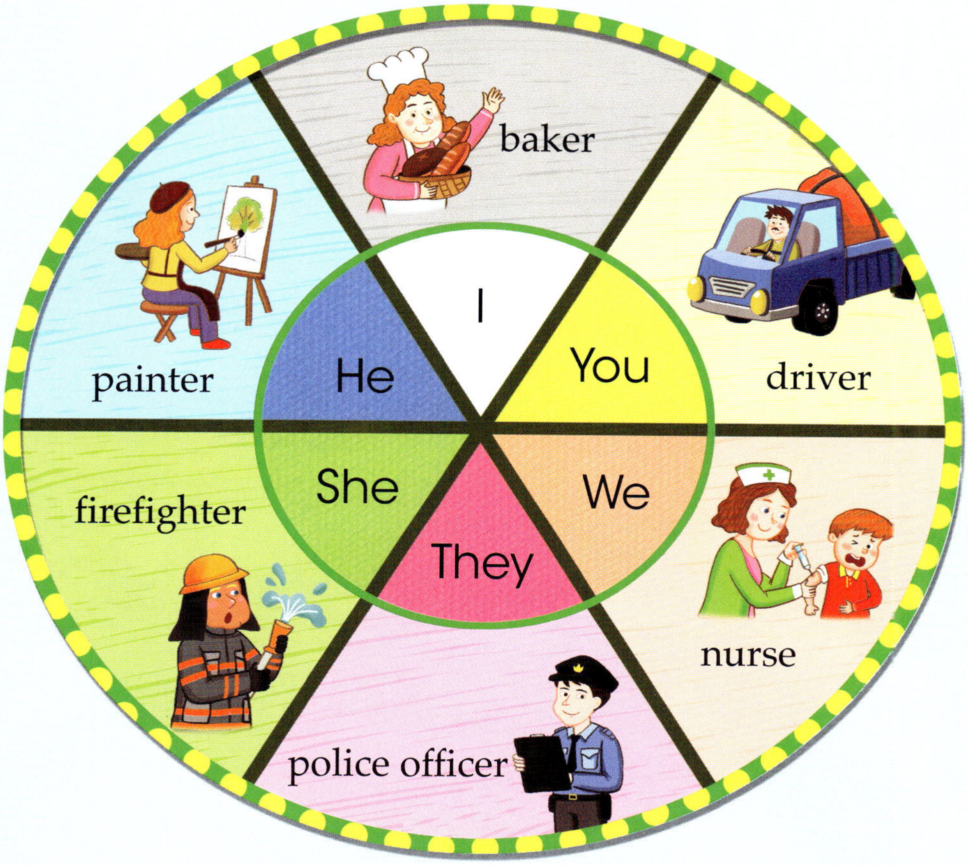

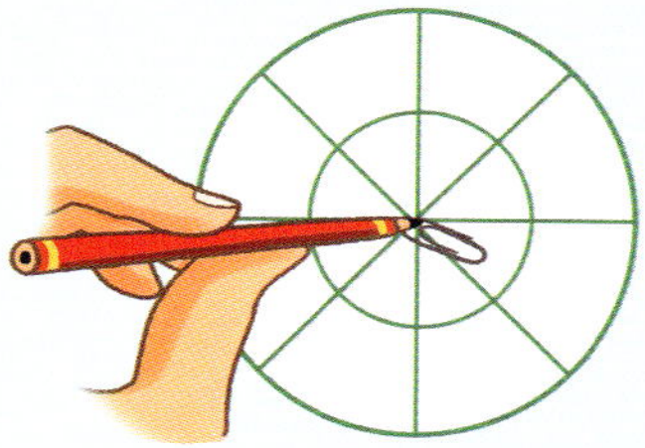

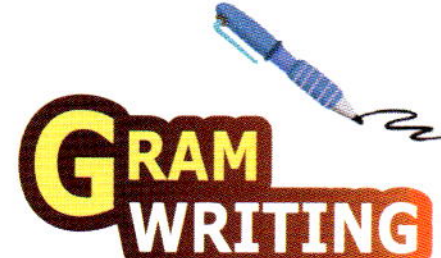

am

is

are

05

GRAM WRITING Correct the mistakes in red and rewrite the sentences.

1 She are a baker. She bakes fresh bread.

2 He are a firefighter. She is a nurse. They is our neighbors.

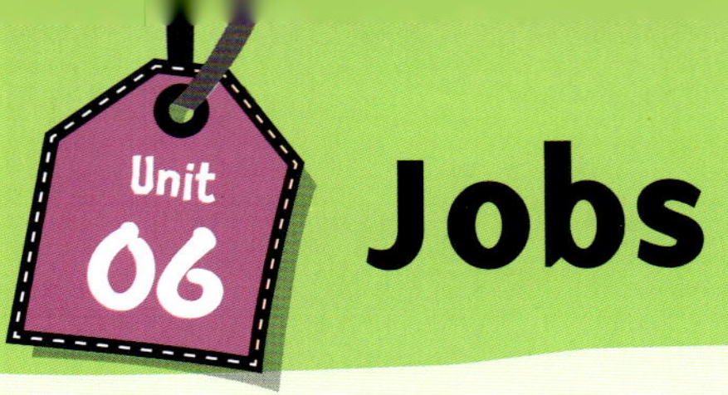

Unit 06

Jobs

Track 16 ☐ Listen ☐ Repeat ☐ Point

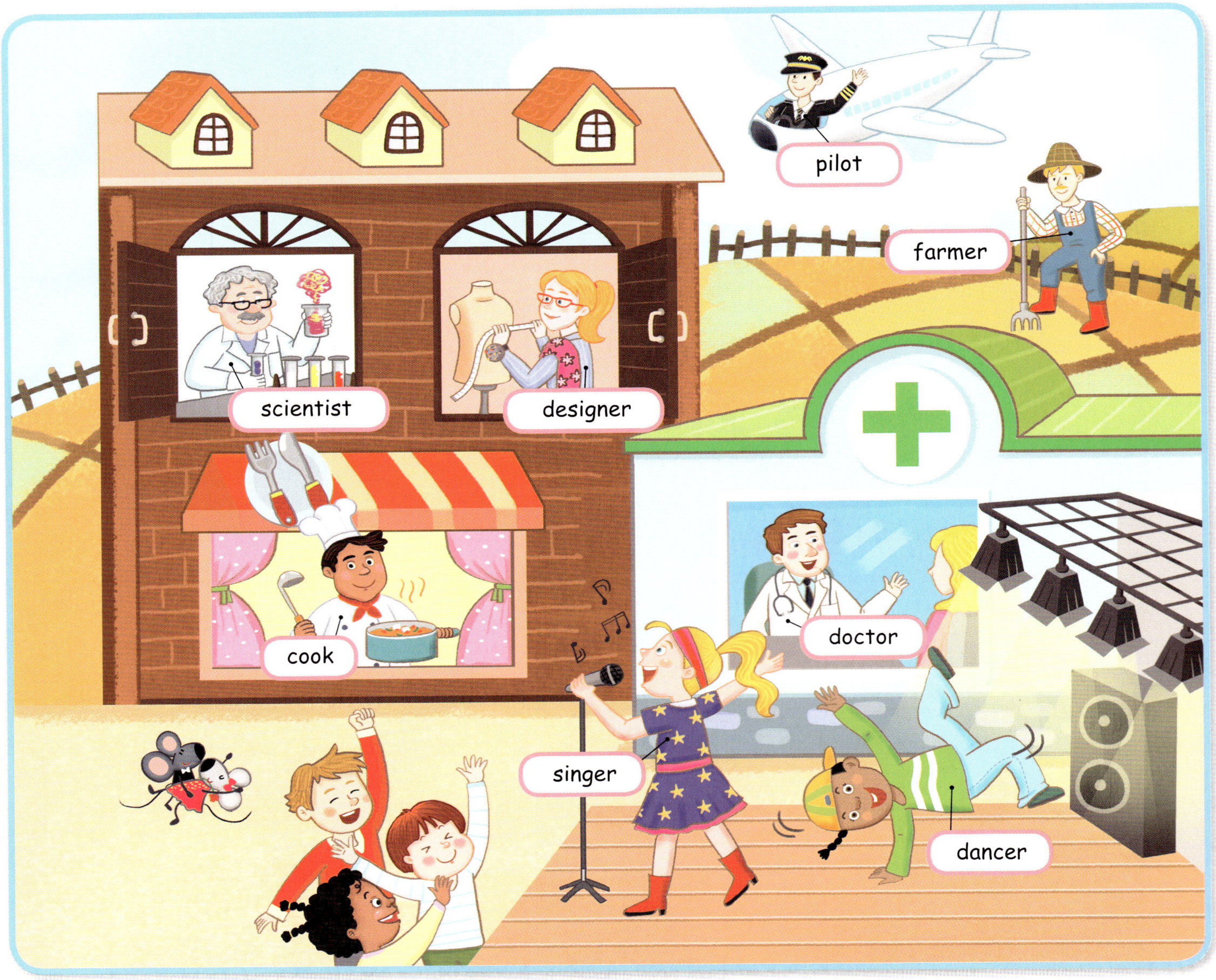

GRAM WORDS ABC

Track 17

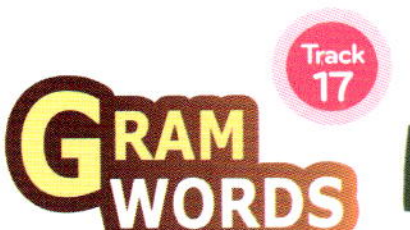

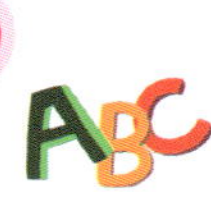

Listen and number the pictures in order. Track 18

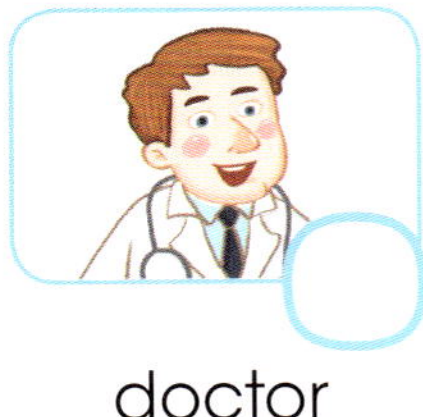

doctor

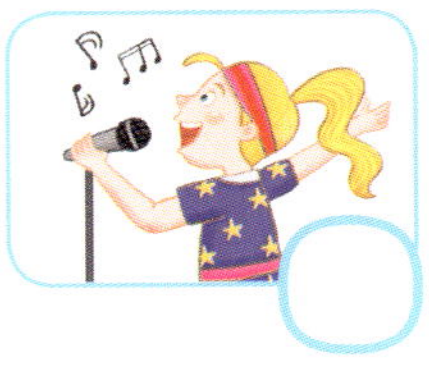

singer

cook

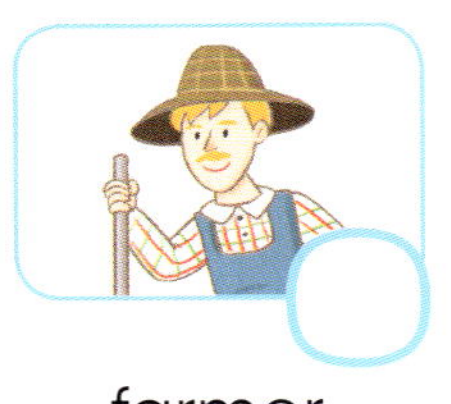

farmer

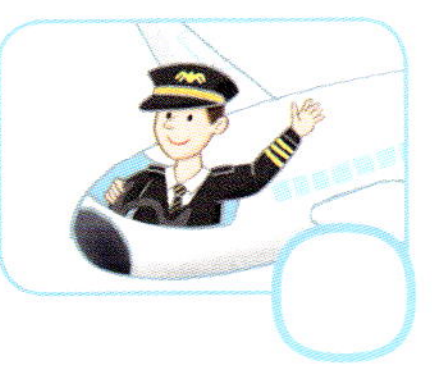

pilot

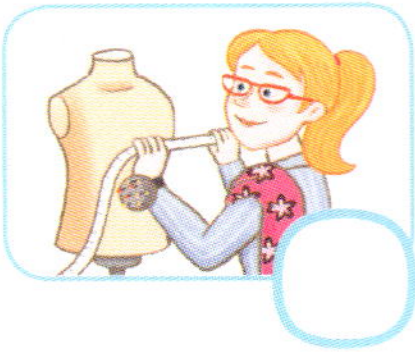

designer

Am / Are / Is + Not

Pronoun + Be verb + not

Singular			Plural		
I	am not	I'm not	We		We aren't
You	are not	You aren't	You		You aren't
He		He isn't	They	are not	
She	is not	She isn't			They aren't
It		It isn't	They		

Examples

- I am not (= I'm not) a doctor.
- She is not (= She isn't) a cook.
- We are not (= We aren't) singers.
- They are not (= They aren't) dancers.

G RAM CHECK UP

Look and write O or X.

1 

We isn't doctors.

2 

I'm not a singer.

3 

They aren't dancers.

4 

He isn't a cook.

5 

He isn't a designer.

6 

You isn't a farmer.

GRAM PRACTICE

A. Match to the correct Be verbs and short forms.

1	I		am not	I'm not
2	She			She isn't
3	He		is not	He isn't
4	You			You aren't
5	They		are not	We aren't
6	We			They aren't

B. Fill in the blanks and trace the words.

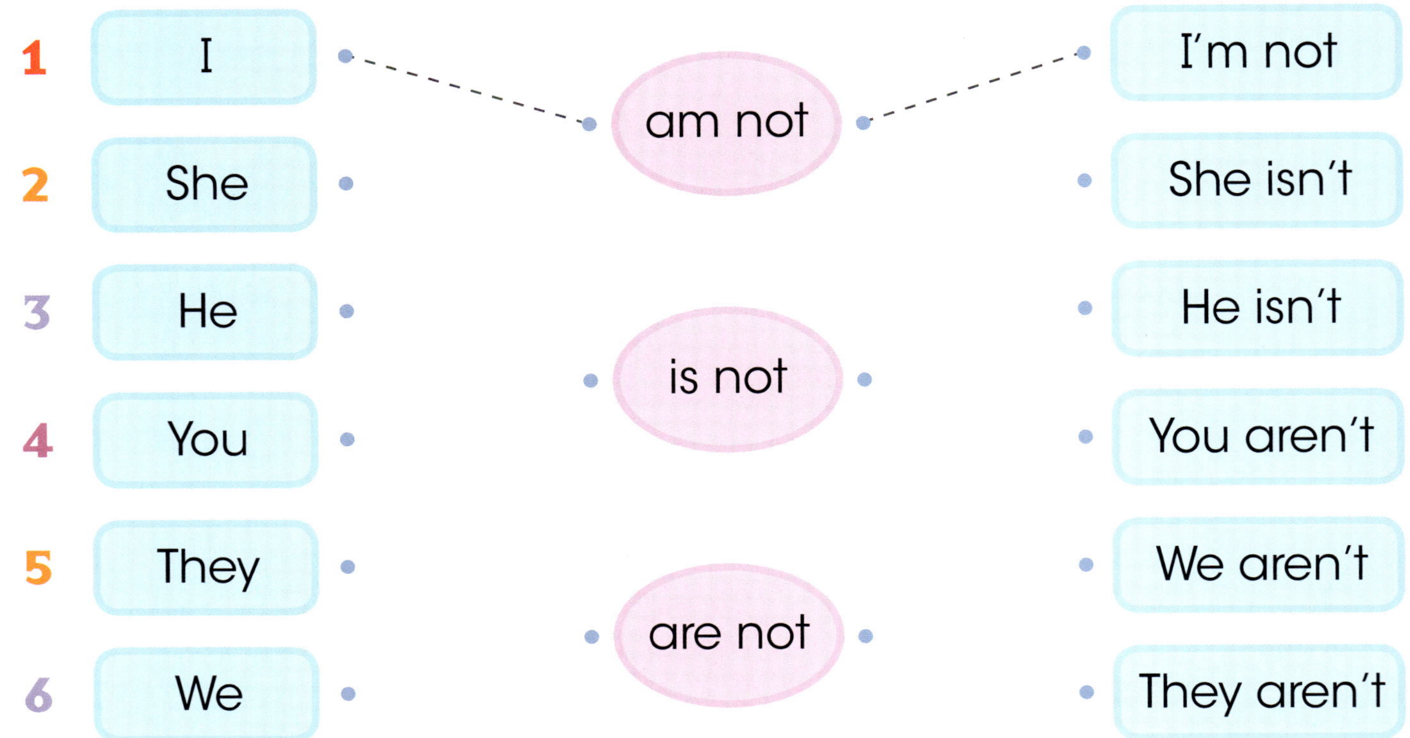

1 She is ____________ a pilot. She is a cook.

2 I __________ not a singer. I am a dancer.

3 They ____________ farmers. They are doctors.

4 He is ____________ a designer. He is a pilot.

5 We ____________ cooks. We are farmers.

Job Board Game

Flick a coin on the board. Move 1 space for heads, 2 spaces for tails.

Then make sentences using the proper pronouns and Be verbs.

For example, *"She is a doctor."* or *"He is not a singer."*

Correct the mistakes in red and rewrite the sentences.

1 I amn't a student. I is a teacher.

2 He aren't a pilot. He is a designer.

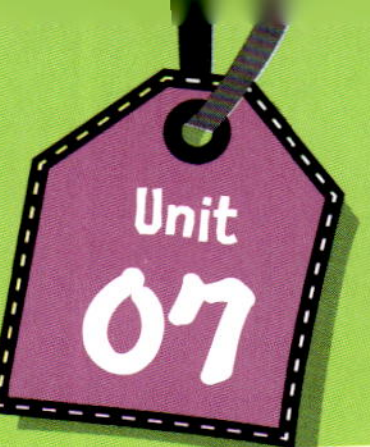

Unit 07

Our Classroom

Track 19 □ Listen □ Repeat □ Point

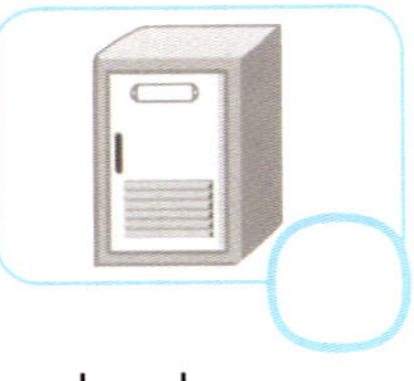

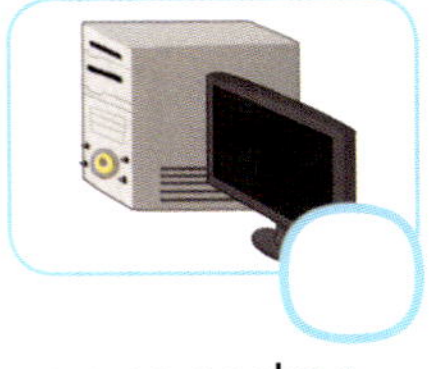

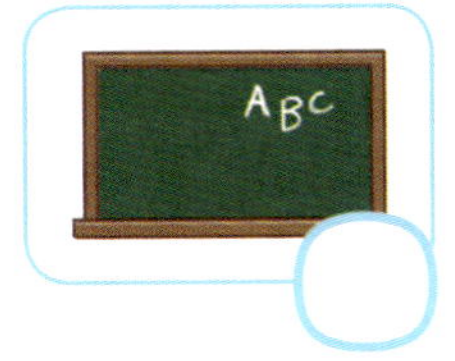

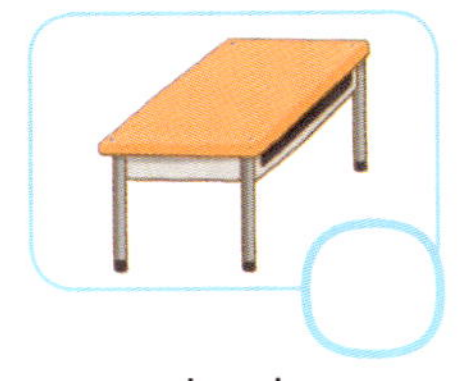

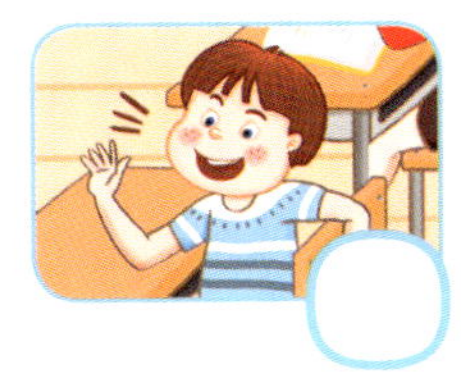

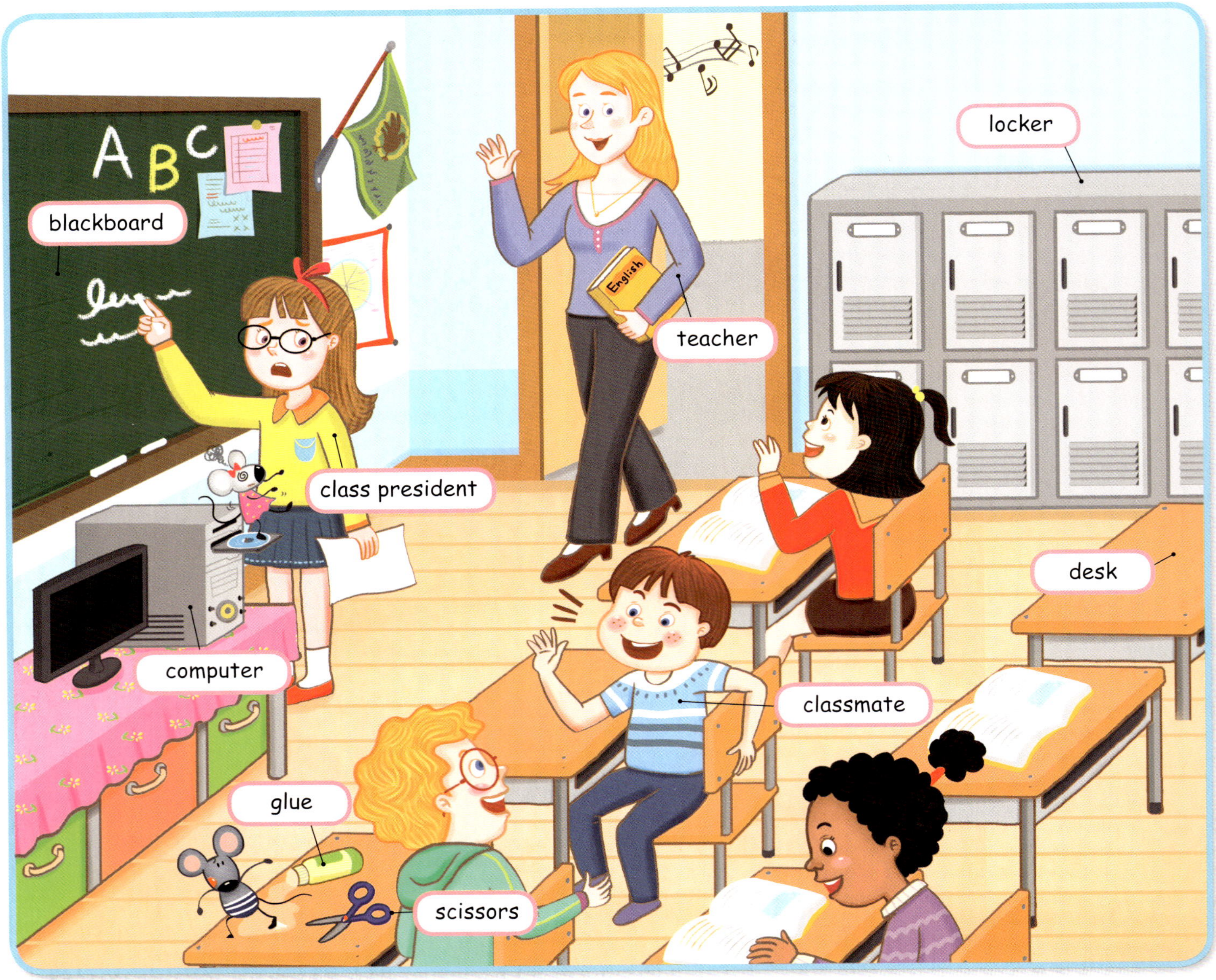

GRAM WORDS ABC Track 20 Listen and number the pictures in order. Track 21

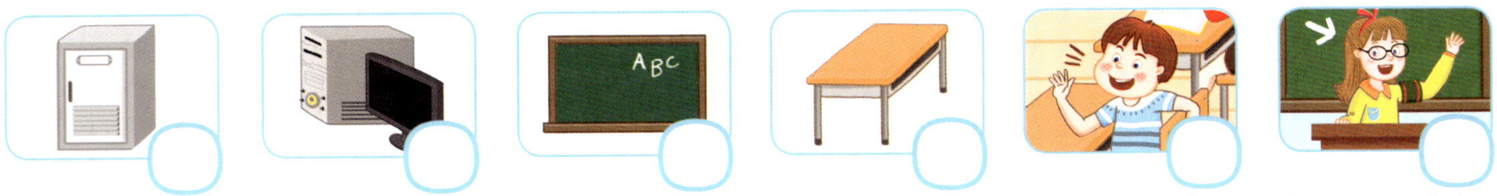

locker | computer | blackboard | desk | classmate | class president

Be verb + Subject ~ ?

Questions			Answers
I	am	Am I ~?	Yes, you are. / No, you aren't.
You	are	Am you ~?	Yes, I am. / No, I'm not.
They		Am they ~?	Yes, they are. / No, they aren't.
We		Am we ~?	Yes, we are. / No, we aren't.
He	is	Is he ~?	Yes, he is. / No, he isn't.
She		Is she ~?	Yes, she is. / No, she isn't.
It		Is it ~?	Yes, it is. / No, it isn't.

07

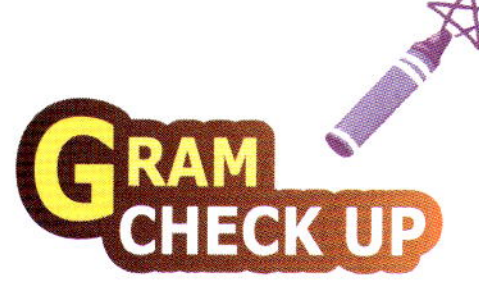

GRAM **CHECK UP**   Circle the correct words.

1 [Are | Is] you a student? – Yes, I am.

2 [Am | Are] they teachers? – Yes, they are.

3 [Is | Are] it a desk? – No, it isn't.

4 [Am | Is] it a glue? – Yes, it is.

5 [Are | Am] we classmates? – Yes, we are.

6 [Am | Is] she your sister? – No, she isn't.

GRAM PRACTICE

A. Look and check the correct answers.

1 Is it a computer?
☐ Yes, it is. ☐ No, it isn't.

2 Are they classmates?
☐ Yes, they are. ☐ No, they aren't.

3 Are you a teacher?
☐ Yes, I am. ☐ No, I'm not.

4 Are they desks?
☐ Yes, they are. ☐ No, they aren't.

B. Read and write the correct words.

Word Box   Are   they   Is   it   he

1 _______ you a girl?

2 _______ she a student?

3 Is _______ Mike?

4 Are _______ your friends?

5 _______ we classmates?

6 _______ you a teacher?

7 _______ it a glue?

8 _______ they scissors?

9 Is _______ an eraser?

10 _______ they teachers?

Ladder Game

Look at the pictures at the bottom of the ladder.

Follow the ladder and make two questions for each of the ladders.

(For example, *"Is it a locker? / Is it a computer?"*)

Correct the mistakes in red and rewrite the sentences.

1 A: Are he the class president?   B: Yes, he are. He is nice.

2 I am a teacher. Am you a student?

Favorite Subjects

☐ **Listen** ☐ **Repeat** ☐ **Point**

math

English

art

social studies

P.E.

history

science

music

Listen and number the pictures in order. Track 24

| math | English | art | history | science | music |

Who / What ~ ?

Who / What + Be verb ~ ?

Who			What		
Who	am	I?	What	is	it?
	is	he / she?		are	they?
	are	you/ we/ they?			

Examples

- Who are you? – I am Jason.
- Who is he? – He is Tom.
- Who are they? – They are Jason and Tom.
- Who is it? – It is a pencil.
- What are they? – They are pencils.

GRAM CHECK UP

Look and circle the correct word.

1 

[Who / What] are you?

2 

[Who / What] is he?

3 

[Who / What] is it?

4 

[Who / What] are they?

5 

[Who / What] is she?

6 

[Who / What] are they?

A. Look and fill in the blanks.

1 

A: __________ is she?
B: She is an English teacher.

2 

A: __________ is he?
B: __________ is my history teacher.

3 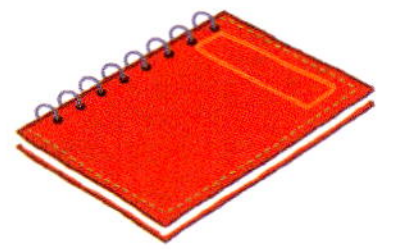

A: __________ is it?
B: It is a notebook.

4 

A: __________ are they?
B: __________ are books.

Who

They

He

What

B. Unscramble the sentences.

1 they / ? / Who / are → ___________________________________

2 is / ? / Who / he → ___________________________________

3 Who / ? / we / are → ___________________________________

4 it / ? / What / is → ___________________________________

5 What / ? / they / are → ___________________________________

6 Who / ? / you / are → ___________________________________

Tic Tac Toe

Make questions and answers using the given hints.

(For example, *Who is she? – She is my English teacher.*)

If you make a sentence, draw an X on the picture if you are player 1, or an O if you are player 2. When you get 4 pictures in a row in any direction, you win the game.

GRAM WRITING Correct the mistakes in red and rewrite the sentences.

1 A: What is she?   B: It is my art teacher. I like her.

2 A: What is they?   B: You are pens and pencils.

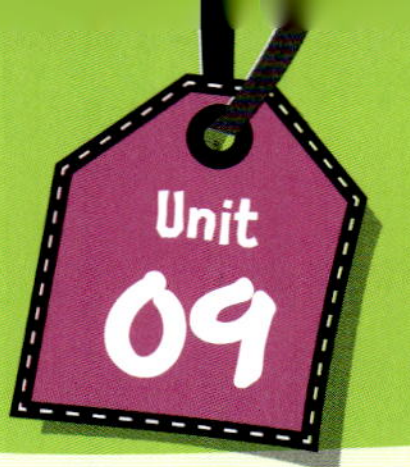

Unit 09

I Am Tall

Track 25 □ Listen □ Repeat □ Point

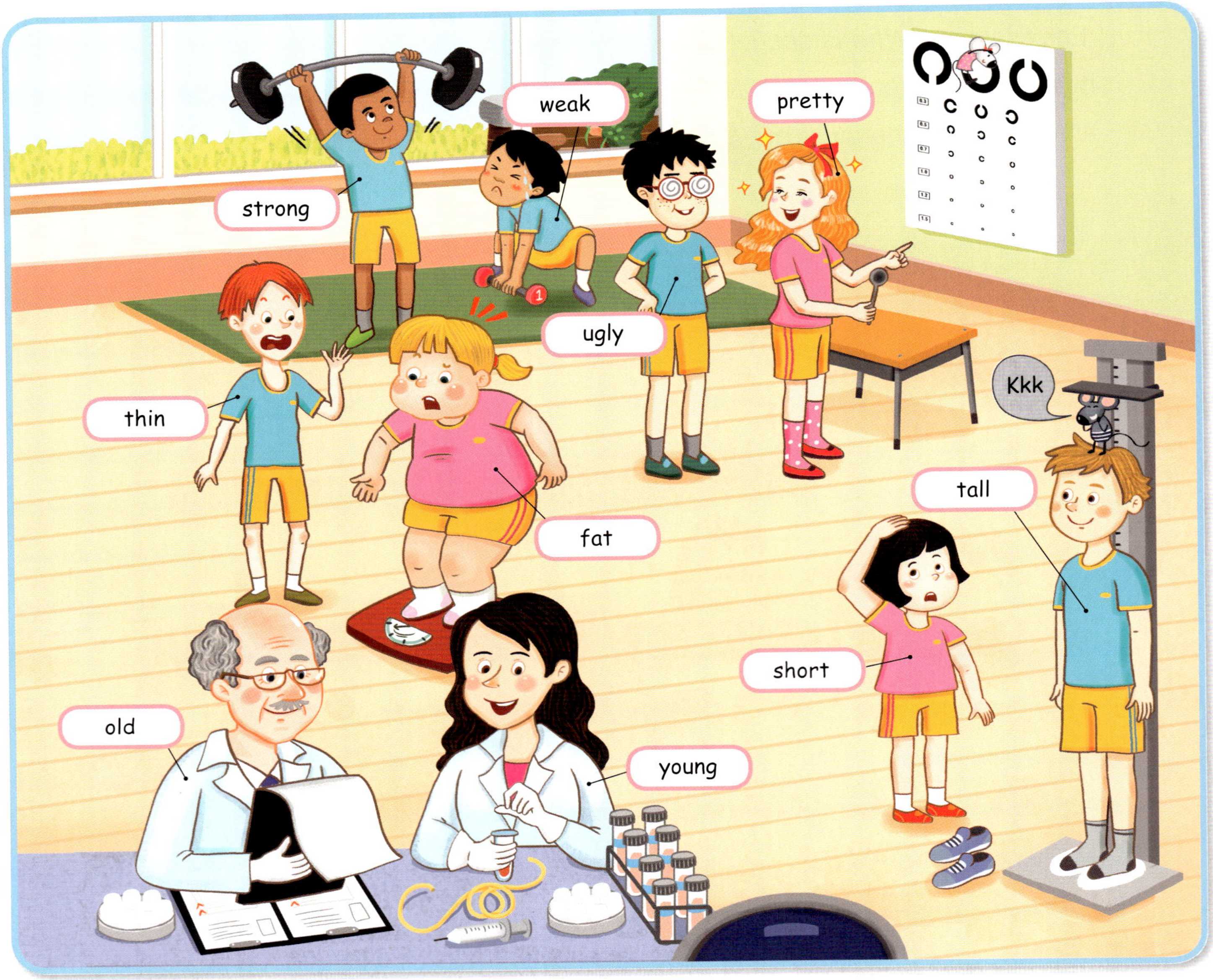

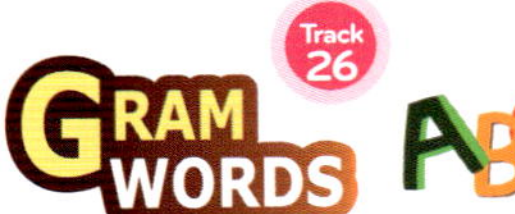

GRAM WORDS Track 26 ABC Listen and number the pictures in order. Track 27

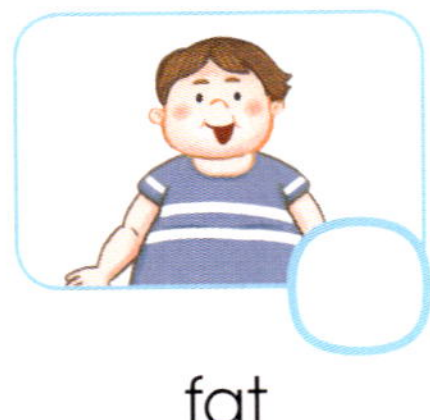

fat thin pretty short tall ugly

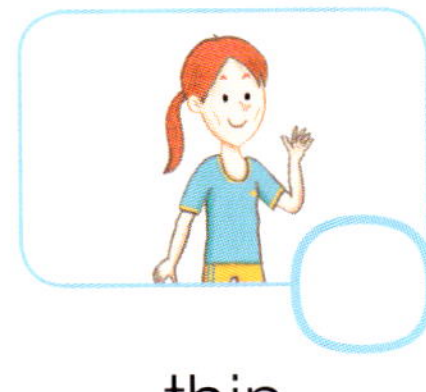

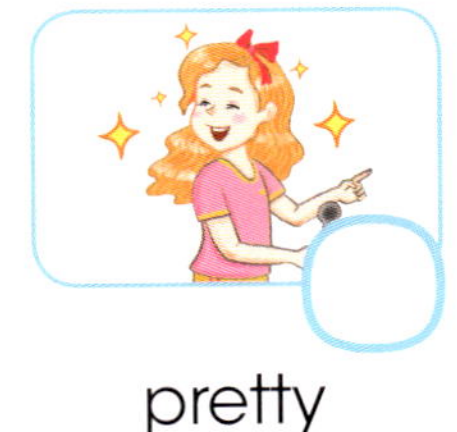

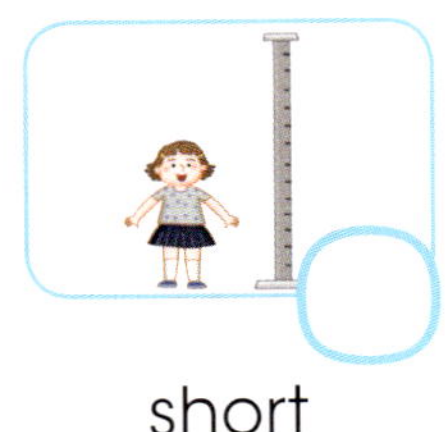

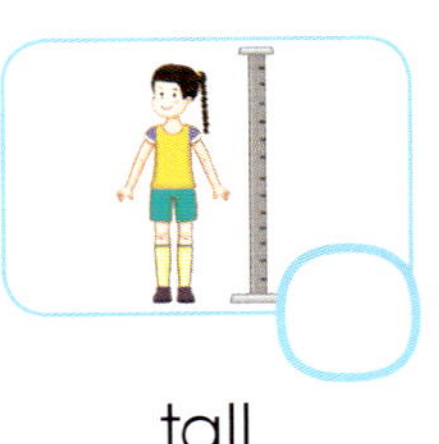

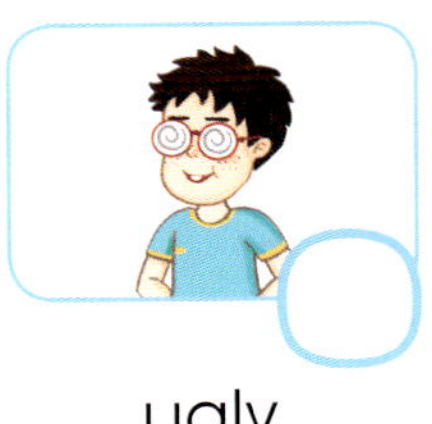

Be + Adjectives (Looks)

Pronouns	Be verbs	Adjectives	
I	I	tall fat pretty strong young	short thin ugly weak old
He / She	is		
You / We / They	are		

Examples

- I am tall.
- He is strong.
- You are pretty.

- You are short.
- She is weak.
- They are old.

GRAM **CHECK UP**   Look and check off the correct word.

1 
☐ tall ☐ short

2 
☐ old ☐ young

3 
☐ fat ☐ thin

4 
☐ strong ☐ weak

5 
☐ pretty ☐ ugly

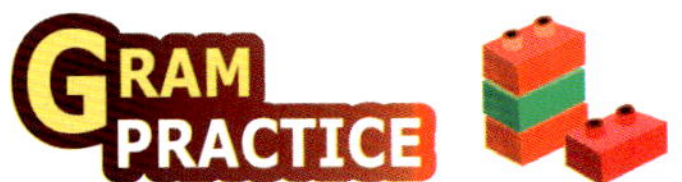

GRAM PRACTICE

A. Complete the words and match them to their opposites.

1

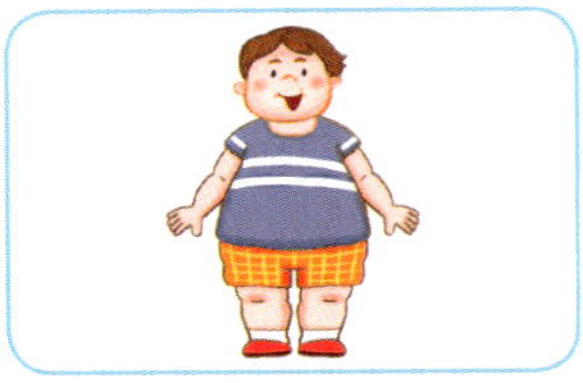

f _ _

2

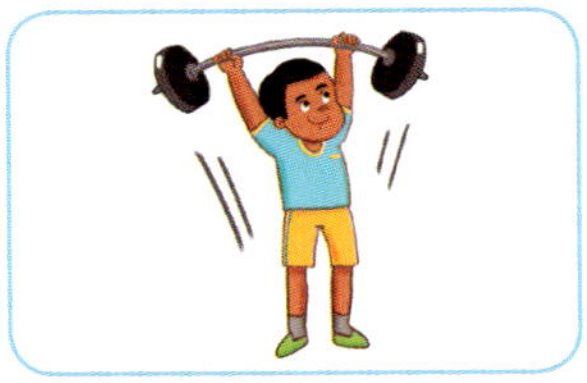

s _ r o _ _

3

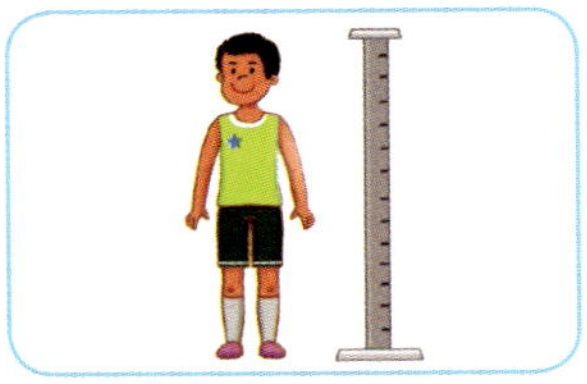

t _ _ _

4

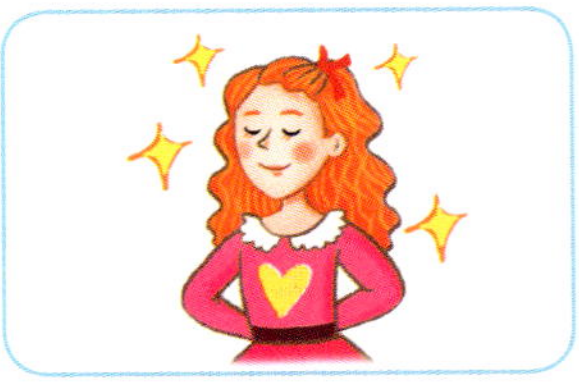

_ _ _ t t _

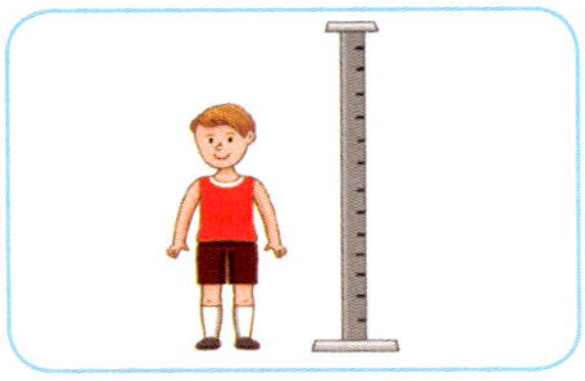

s h _ _ _

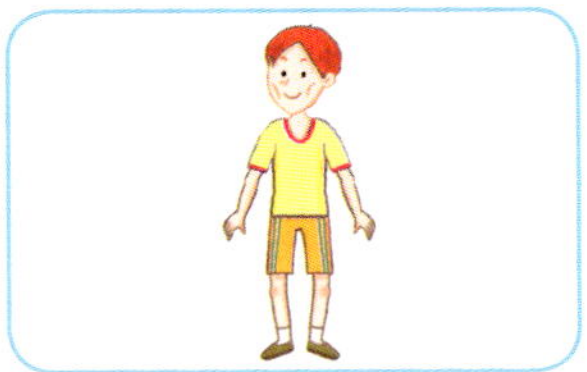

t _ i _

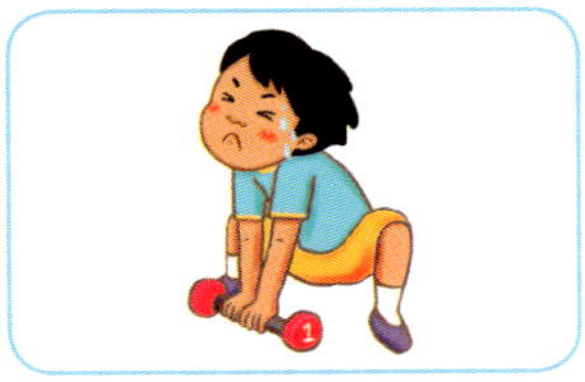

_ _ _ k

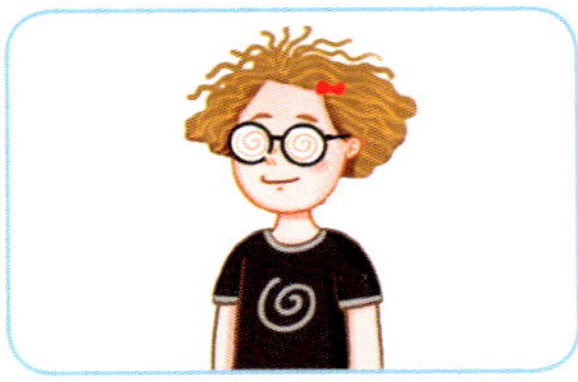

u _ _ y

B. Look and fill in the blanks.

short strong tall thin young fat old weak

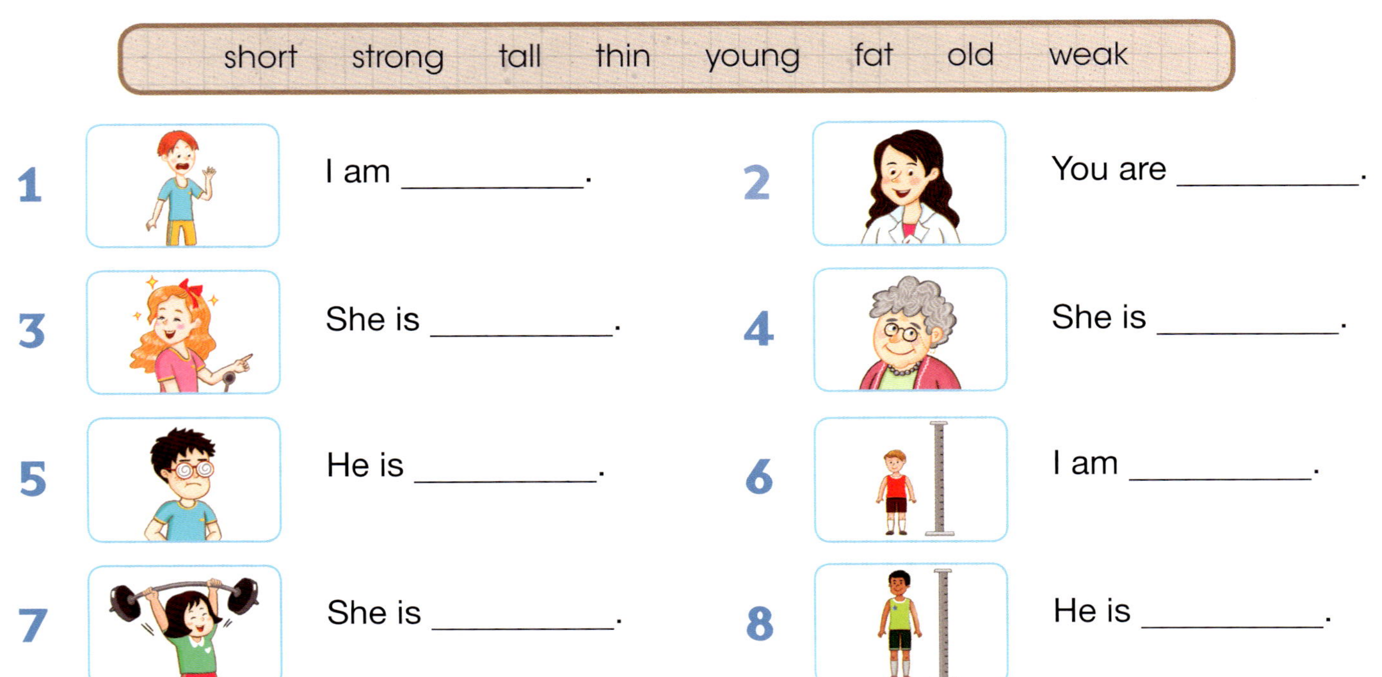

1 I am ________.

2 You are ________.

3 She is ________.

4 She is ________.

5 He is ________.

6 I am ________.

7 She is ________.

8 He is ________.

One player thinks of a card and the other player can ask only Yes or No questions. They have 20 questions to guess who SHE is.

fat / short

pretty / tall

ugly / weak

old / strong

tall / young

fat / tall

weak / short

thin / strong

GRAM WRITING **Correct the mistakes in red and rewrite the sentences.**

1 Steve is not thinn. He are fat.

____

2 Jenny are short and Amy is tail.

____

Unit 10

Jake Is Angry

Track 28 □ Listen □ Repeat □ Point

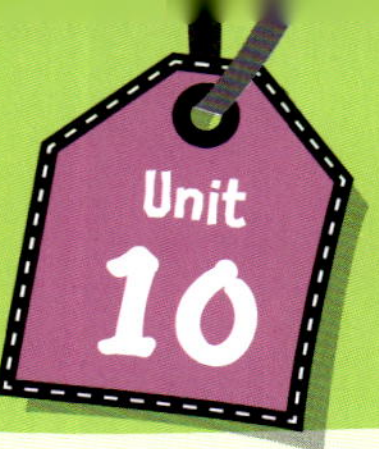

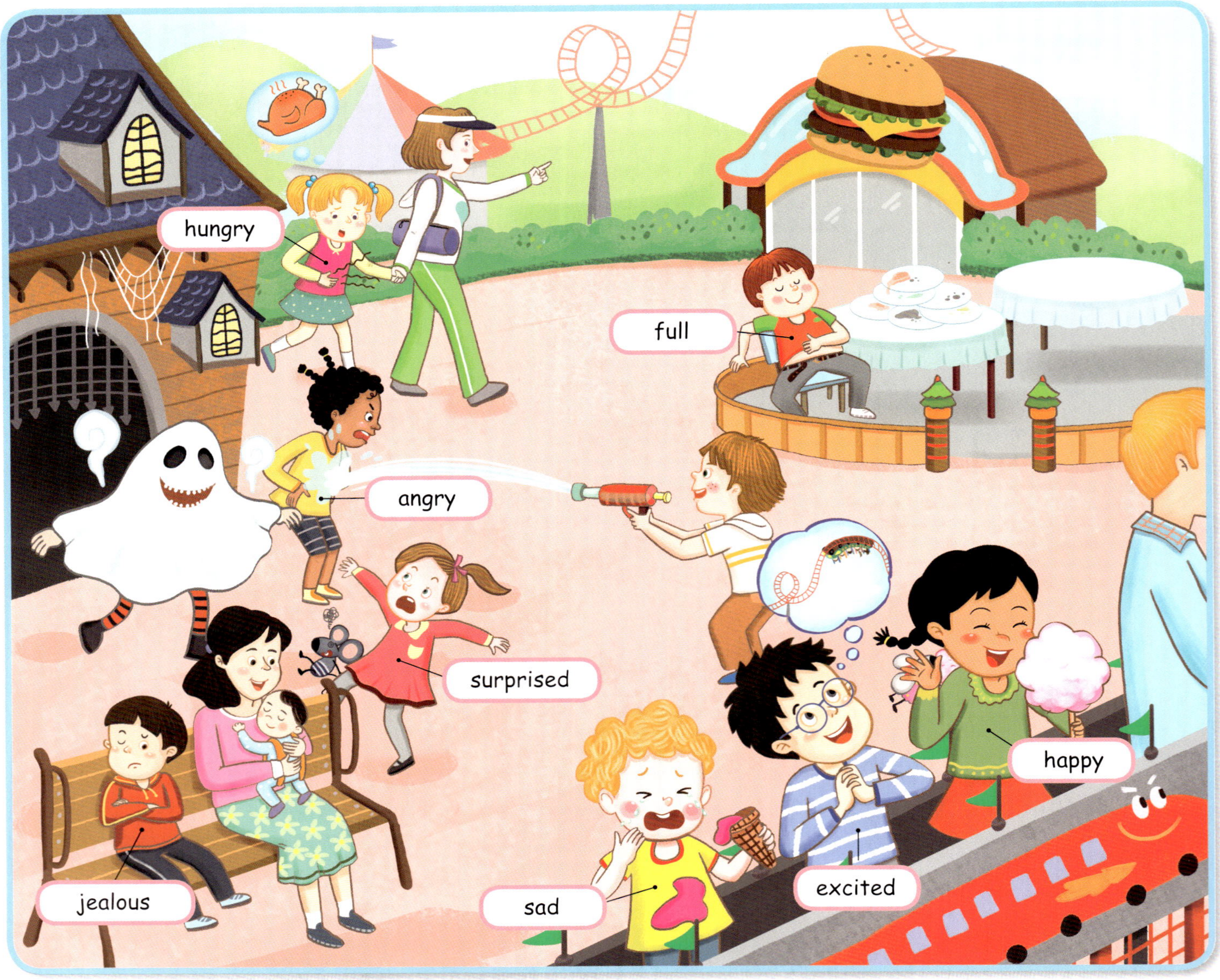

GRAM WORDS Track 29 ABC Listen and number the pictures in order. Track 30

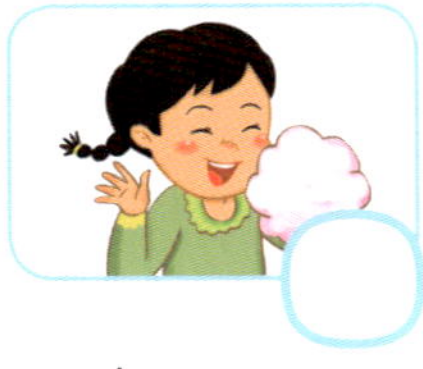

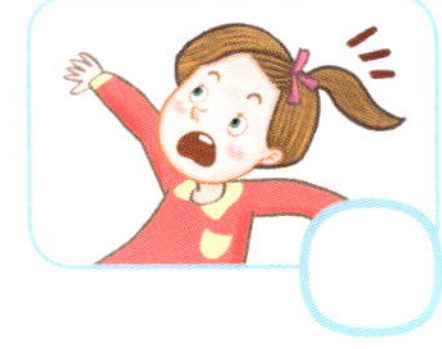

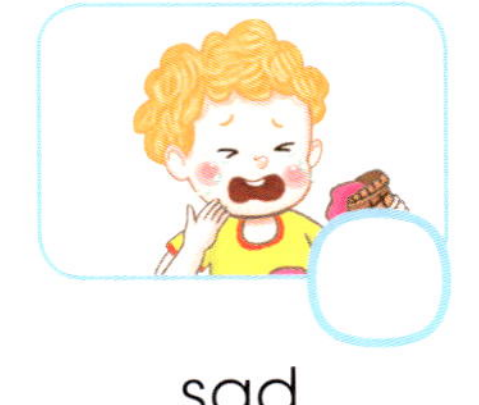

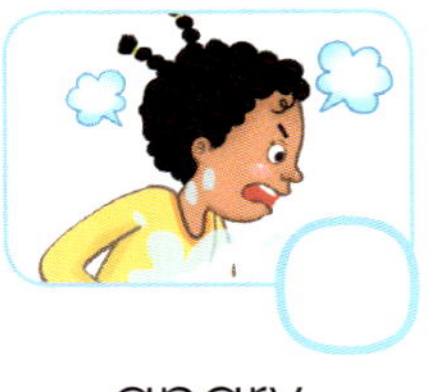

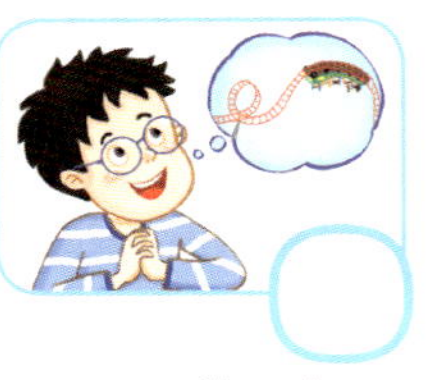

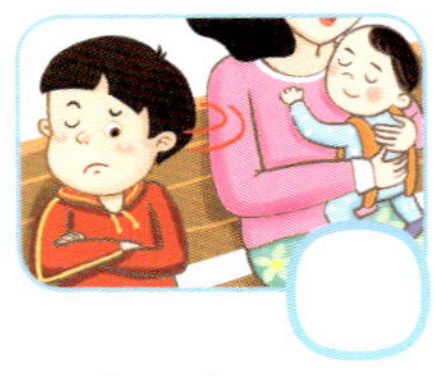

happy

surprised

sad

angry

excited

jealous

Be + Adjectives (Feelings)

Pronouns	Be verbs	Adjectives	
I	am	happy sad surprised hungry	angry excited jealous full
He / She	is		
You / We / They	are		

Examples

- I am happy.
- He is excited.
- You are hungry.

- You are sad.
- She is jealous.
- They are full.

10

GRAM **CHECK UP**  Look and check off the correct word.

1 

☐ happy ☐ sad

2 

☐ sad ☐ angry

3 

☐ full ☐ surprised

4 

☐ angry ☐ hungry

5 

☐ angry ☐ excited

6 

☐ jealous ☐ happy

A. Fill in the blanks.

> hungry   sad   happy   excited   jealous   angry   full   surprised

1   I am __________.

2   You are __________.

3   He is __________.

4   He is __________.

5   He is __________.

6   They are __________.

7   He is __________.

8   She is __________.

B. Unscramble and rewrite the sentences.

1   She / . / happy / is   → ______________________________

2   full / I / . / am   → ______________________________

3   . / hungry / I / am   → ______________________________

4   are / They / excited / .   → ______________________________

5   You / angry / are / .   → ______________________________

6   is / He / . / surprised   → ______________________________

Flick & Draw

Flick a coin and see where it lands. Draw a face in the square the coin landed.

Then, ask a question and answer it.

(For example, *"Is he happy? – Yes, he is. / No, he isn't."*)

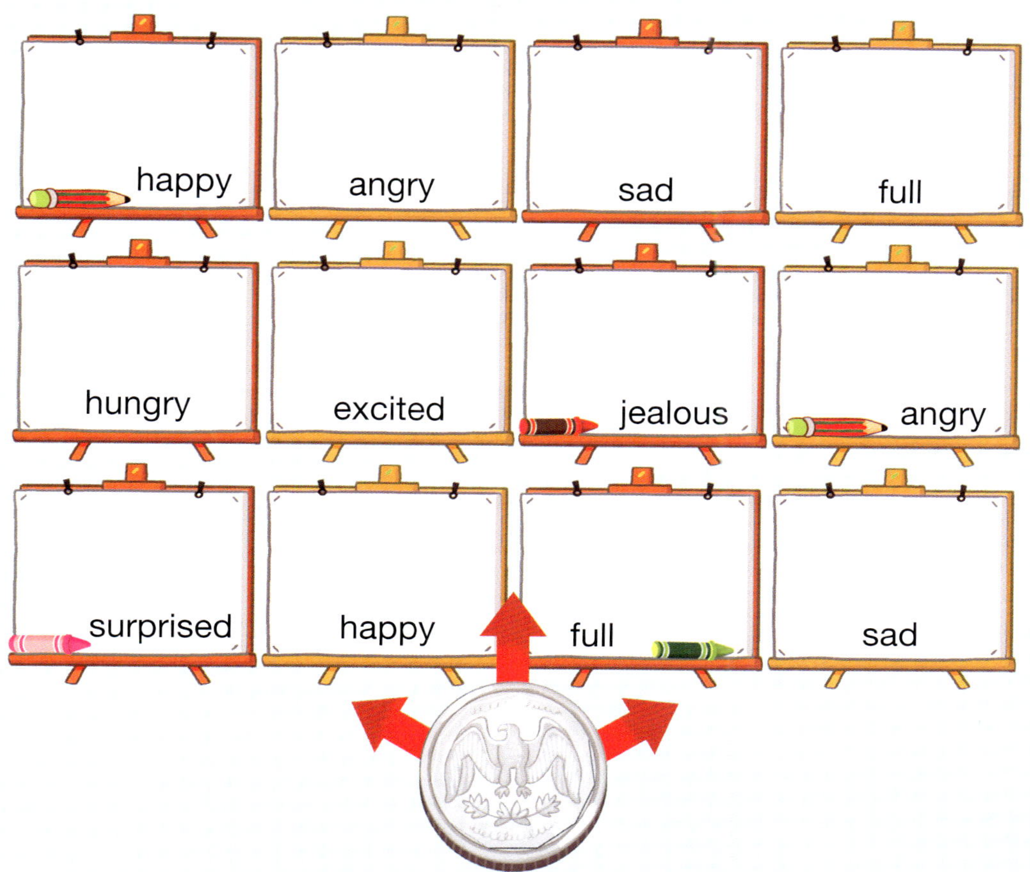

Correct the mistakes in red and rewrite the sentences.

1   Is you happy? – Yes, I is happy.

2   Are they hangry? – No, you are full.

Unit 11

It Is A Red Balloon

Track 31 □ Listen □ Repeat □ Point

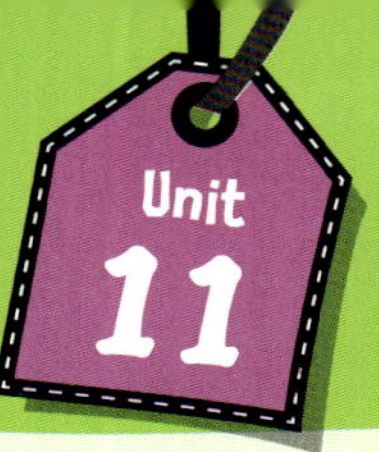

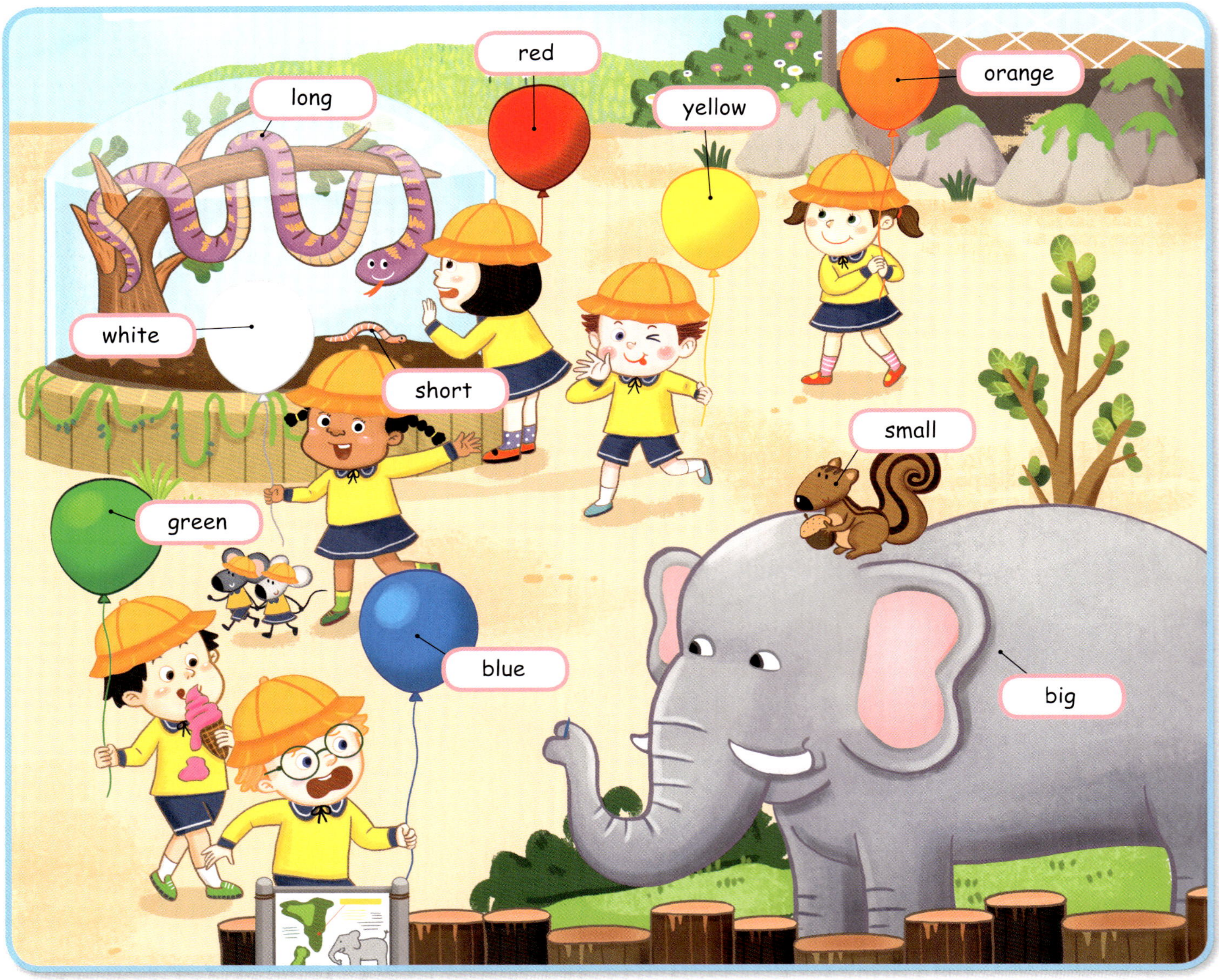

GRAM WORDS Track 32 ABC Listen and number the pictures in order. Track 33

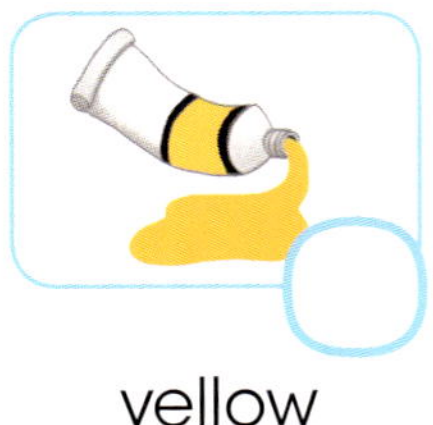

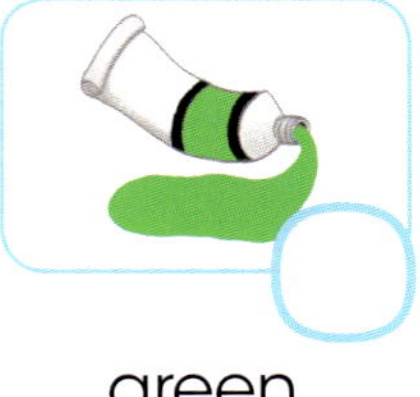

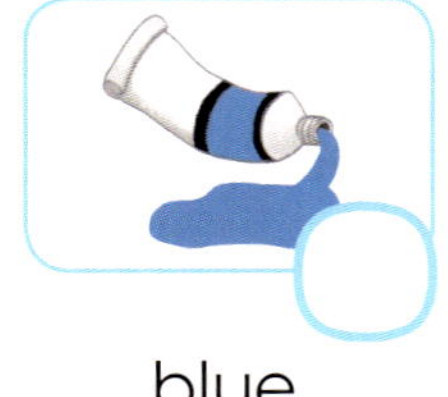

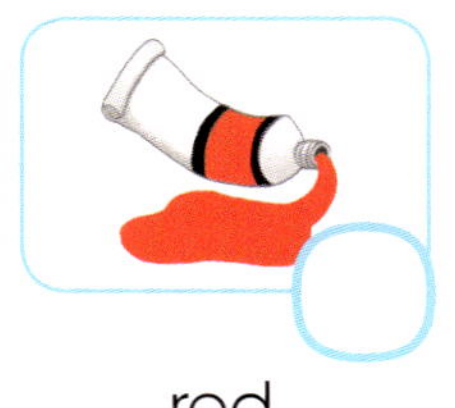

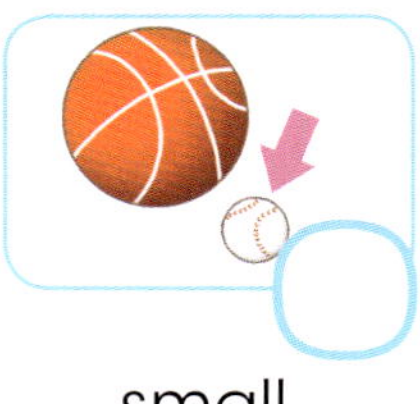

yellow	green	blue	red	long	small

Be + Adjectives (Colors / Sizes)

Be + Adjective	Adjective + Noun
The <u>balloon</u> is red.	It is a red balloon.
=	
The socks are green.	They are green socks.
The elephant is big.	It is a big elephant.
The snake is long.	It is a long snake.

Examples

- The mouse is small. = It is a small mouse.
- The bag is blue. = It is a blue bag.

GRAM CHECK UP   Look and check the correct word.

1 

☐ blue balloon
☐ red balloon

2 

☐ long snake
☐ short snake

3 

☐ yellow pants
☐ green pants

4 

☐ big tiger
☐ small tiger

5 

☐ orange bag
☐ white bag

6 

☐ small flower
☐ big flower

GRAM PRACTICE

A. Fill in the blanks.

1  The pig is big. = It is a _________ _________.

2  The _________ is _________. = It is a yellow balloon.

3  The pencil is long. = It is a _________ _________.

4  The flower is red. = It is a _________ _________.

5  The bag is _________. = It is a small _________.

B. Change each sentence like the example shown.

> It is a green ball. → The ball is green.

1 It is a long pencil. → ______________________________

2 It is a small cup. → ______________________________

3 It is a red skirt. → ______________________________

4 It is a white bag. → ______________________________

5 It is a big lion. → ______________________________

6 It is a green hat. → ______________________________

Matching Game

Read each sentence. Write the number that matches the sentence to the correct picture. Then say the sentences.

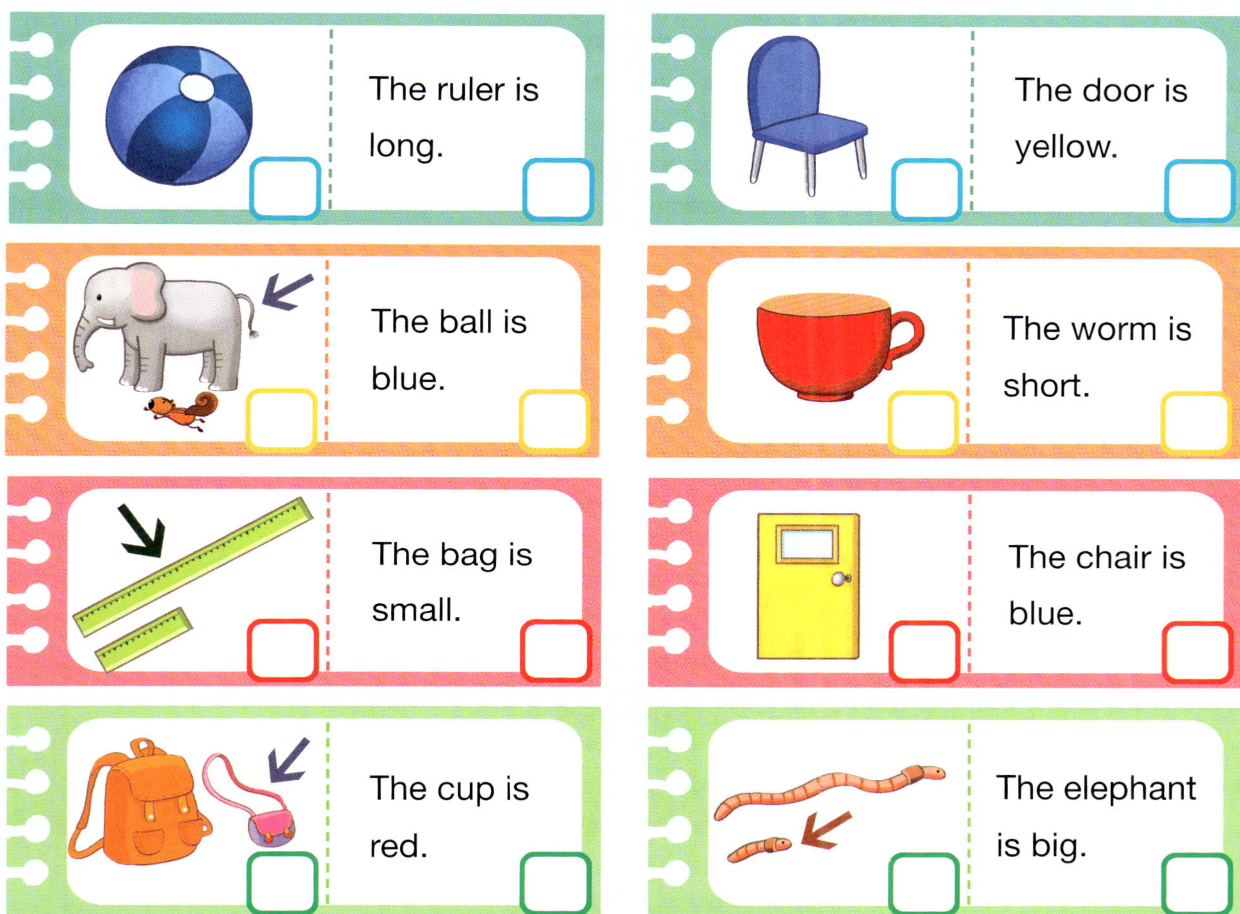

GRAM WRITING Correct the mistakes in red and rewrite the sentences.

1 It is a flower yellow. It is beautiful.

____

2 The elephant big is. It is very big.

____

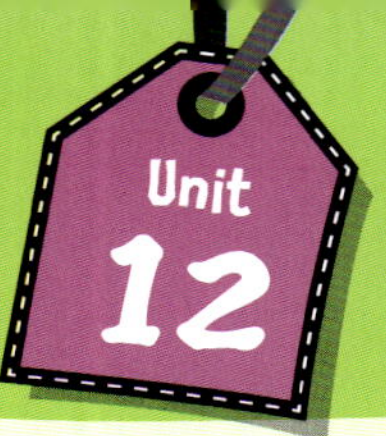

Unit 12

This Is My Hat

Track 34 □ Listen □ Repeat □ Point

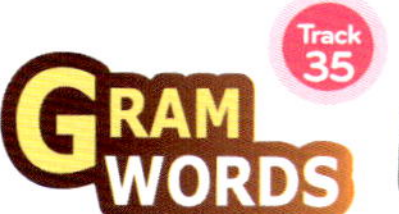

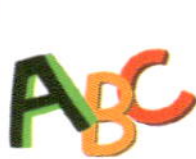

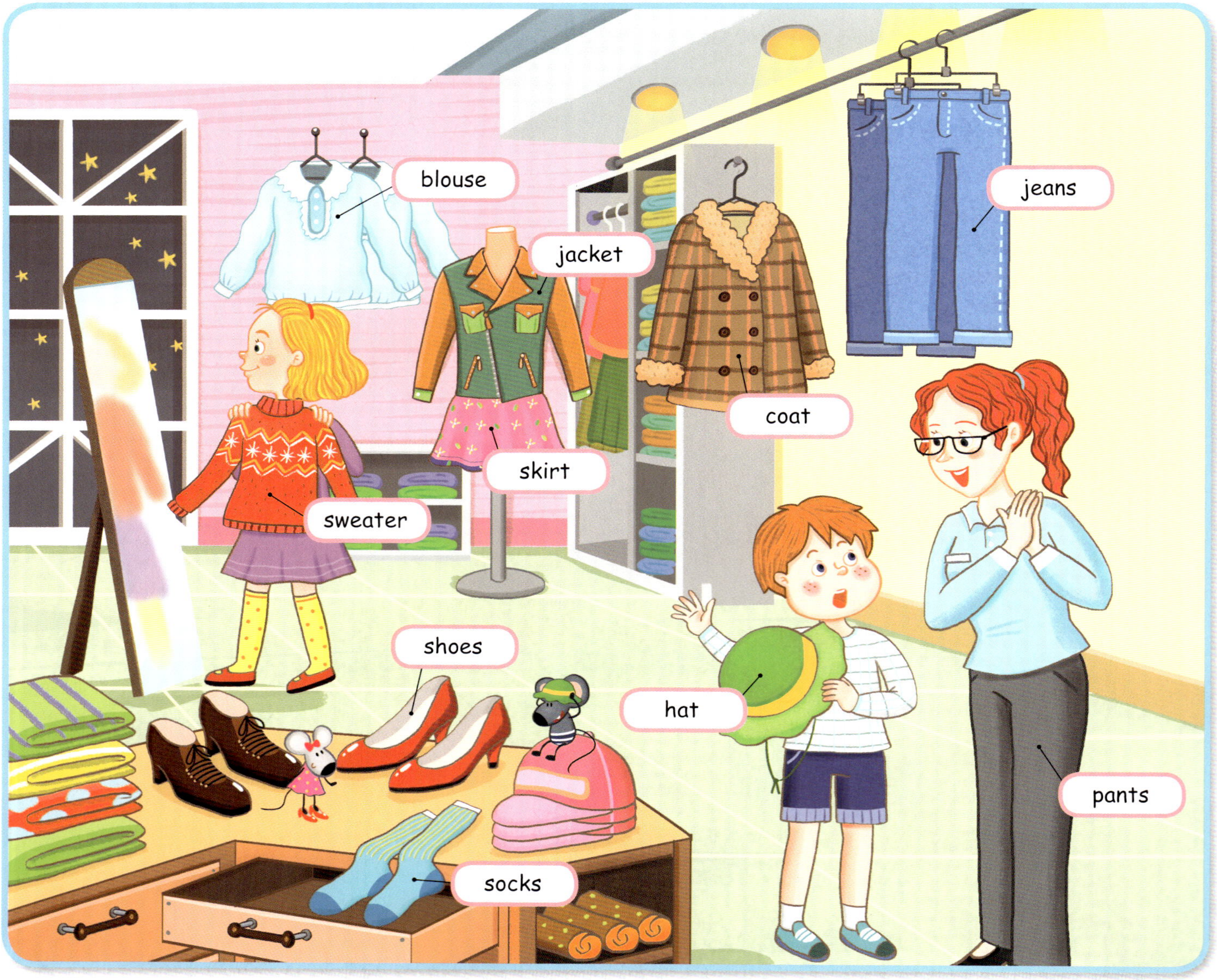

GRAM WORDS Track 35 ABC Listen and number the pictures in order. Track 36

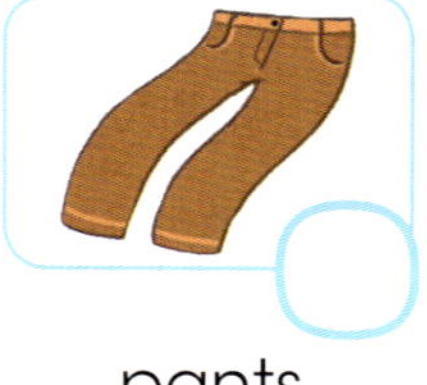

pants

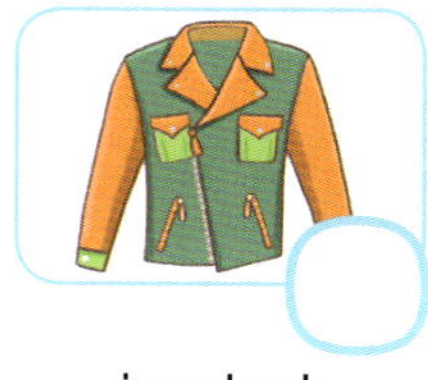

jacket

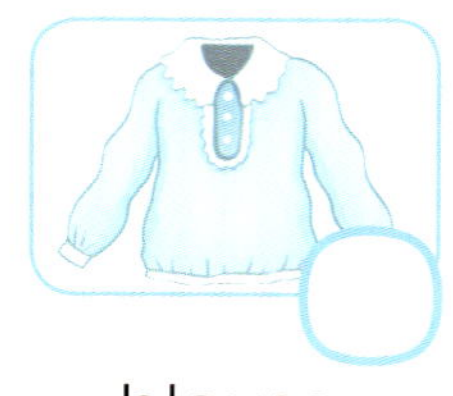

blouse

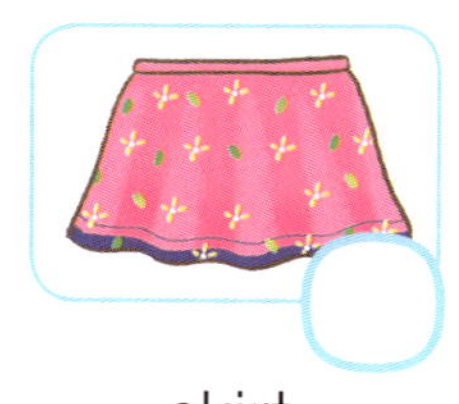

skirt

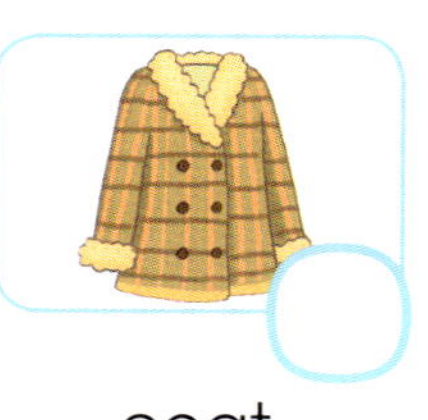

coat

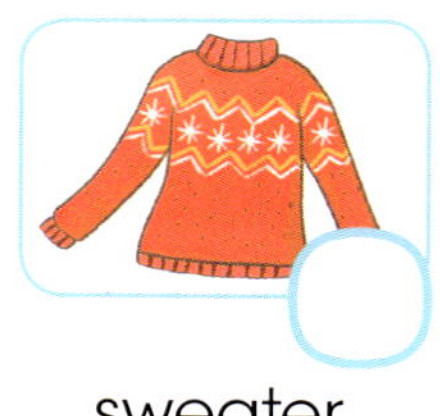

sweater

Possessive Adjectives

Pronouns	Possessive Adjectives	Pronouns	Possessive Adjectives
I	my	it	its
you	your	we	our
he	his	they	their
she	her	Mike	Mike's

Examples

- This is my hat.
- This is her skirt.
- This is his sweater.
- This is their pants.

GRAM **CHECK UP**   Look and write O or X.

1

her jeans

2

her hat

3

my coat

4

your jacket

5

my shoes

6

Jane's skirt

GRAM PRACTICE

A. Match the correct puzzle pieces.

1 he — its
2 you — our
3 she — my
4 they — their
5 it — his
6 we — your
7 I — her
8 Jane — Jane's

B. Circle and write the correct word.

1 This is __________ jacket.

[my / your]

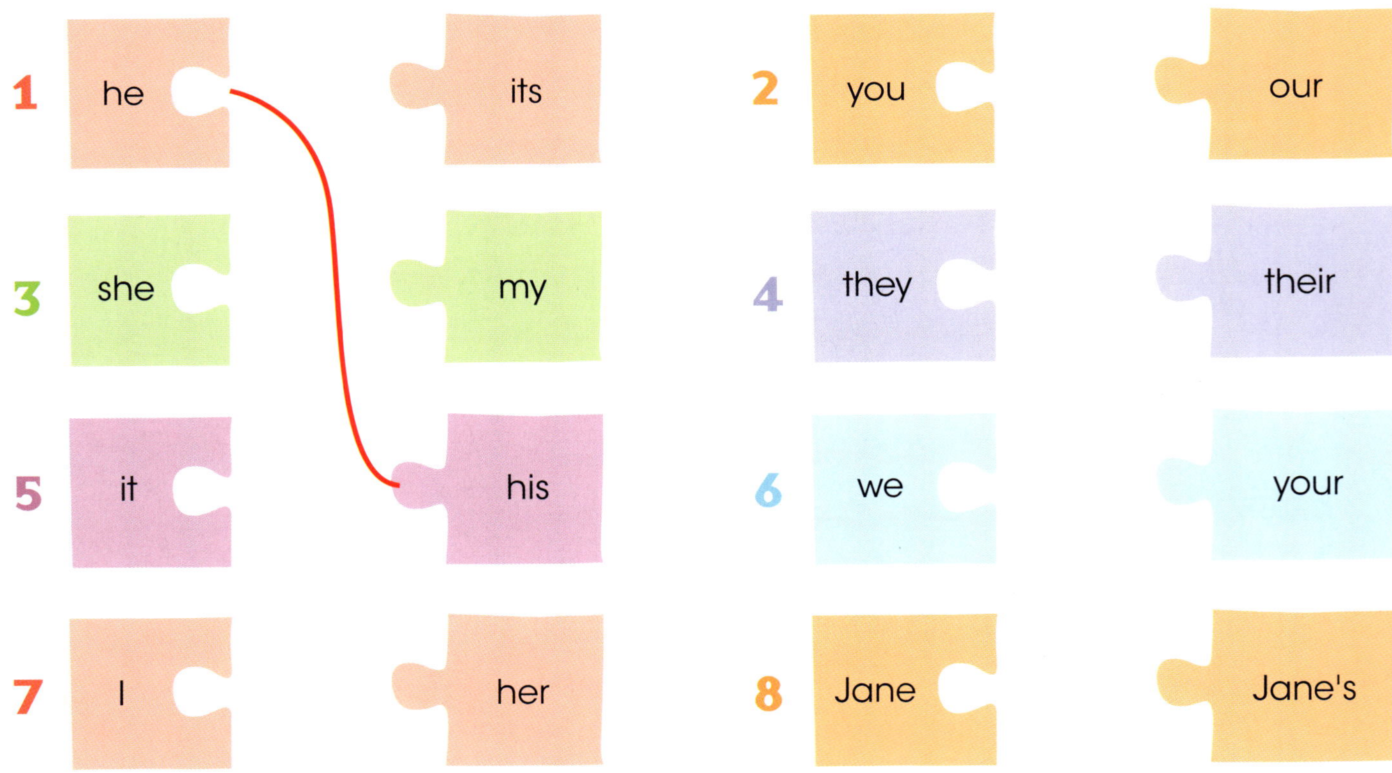

2 This is __________ skirt.

[his / her]

3 This is __________ blouse.

[your / our]

4 This is __________ classroom.

[our / its]

Bingo Game

Cut out the die and glue it together. Roll the word die. Try and make a sentence using the word and picture from the bingo card.

(For example, *It is my hat.*)

If you get 5 pictures in a row in any direction, just yell "BINGO!"

GRAM WRITING Correct the mistakes in red and rewrite the sentences.

1 This is me jacket. I love it.

____

2 Is this yours coat? It looks nice.

____

This Is A Pear

☐ **Listen**   ☐ **Repeat**   ☐ **Point**

GRAM**WORDS**

A**B**C   **Listen and number the pictures in order.**

strawberry	cherry	kiwi	watermelon	grapes	pear

this : close to us

that: far from us

Statement			Question		
This	is (not)	a pear.	Is	this	a pear?
That				that	

하나의 물건을 가리킬 때 물건의 이름 대신에 사용하는 말로 'this(이것)'와 'that(저것)'이 있어. 가까이 있는 물건에는 'this'를 멀리 있는 물건에는 'that'을 사용하지. '이것(저것)은 ~이다.'라고 말할 때는 'This(That) is ~.' 라고 표현해. 부정문은 'is' 뒤에 'not'을 붙여 'This(that) is not ~.'이라고 하면 된단다.

Examples

- This is a watermelon
- This is not a watermelon.
- Is this a kiwi? - Yes, it is. / No, it isn't.

GRAM CHECK UP

Look and write O or X.

1

This is

2

These are

3

That is

4

This is

5

That is

6

That is

GRAM PRACTICE

A. Look and match.

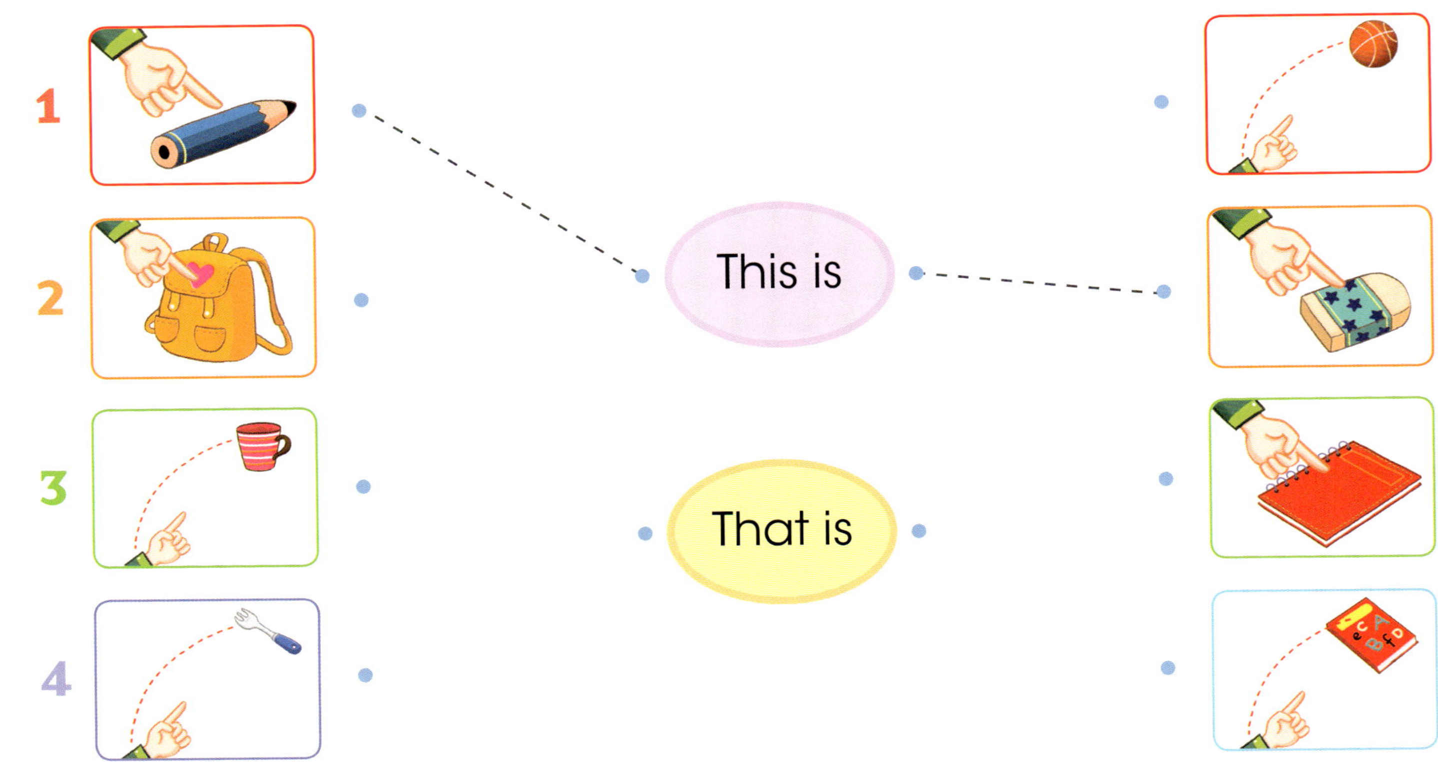

B. Fill in the blanks and circle the correct word.

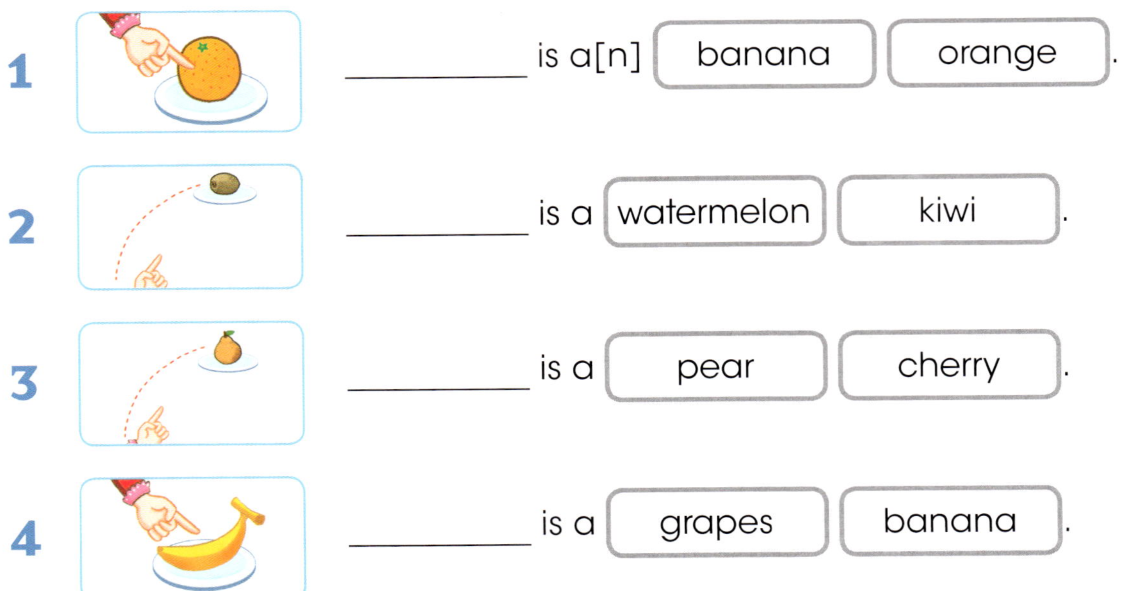

Maze

Follow the pattern (□ ○ 🍓) to find your way out.
Then, say the sentences like in the example.
(*For example, "This is a strawberry."*)

□ This ■ That ○ is
🍓 *name of a fruit*

GRAM **WRITING** Correct the mistakes in red and rewrite the sentences.

1 This are a kiwi. I love kiwis.

2 Look over there. This is a tree.

Those Are Onions

☐ **Listen**   ☐ **Repeat**   ☐ **Point**

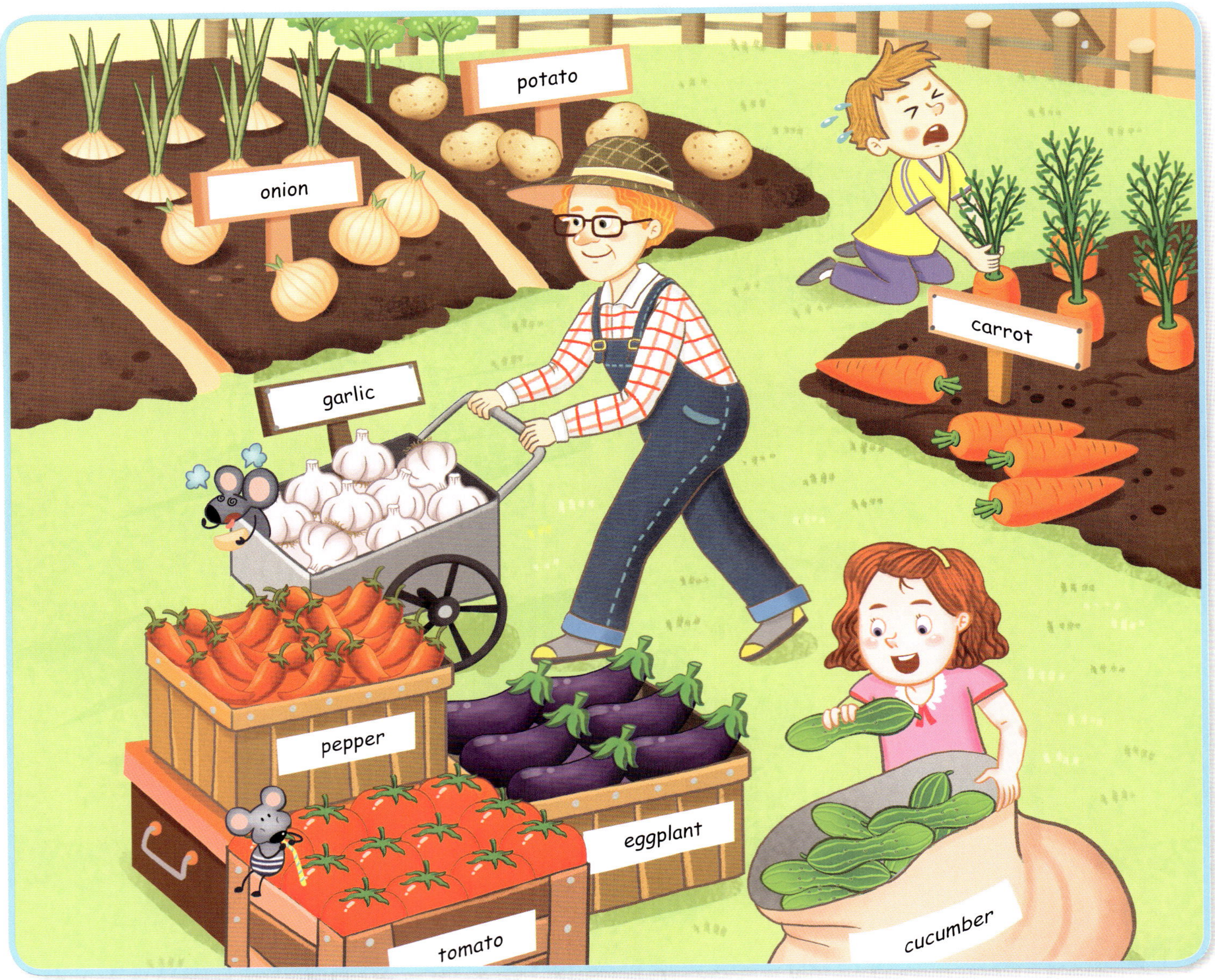

GRAM WORDS

 **ABC**   Listen and number the pictures in order.

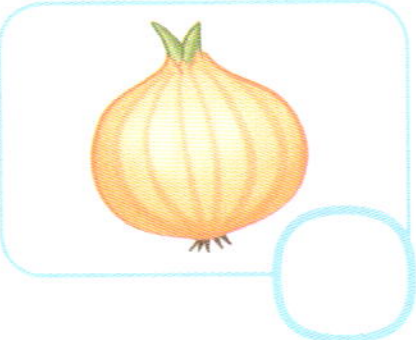

onion	tomato	potato	eggplant	cucumber	carrot

  **These Are / Those Are**

these : close to us

those: far from us

Statement			Question		
These	are (not)	onions.	Are	these	onions?
Those				those	

Examples

- These are potatoes.
- These are not carrots.
- Are these tomatoes? - Yes, they are. / No, they aren't.

GRAM **CHECK UP**   Look and write O or X.

1  ◯

These are

2  ◯

Those are

3  ◯

That are

4  ◯

These are

5  ◯

These is

6  ◯

Those are

A. Look and match.

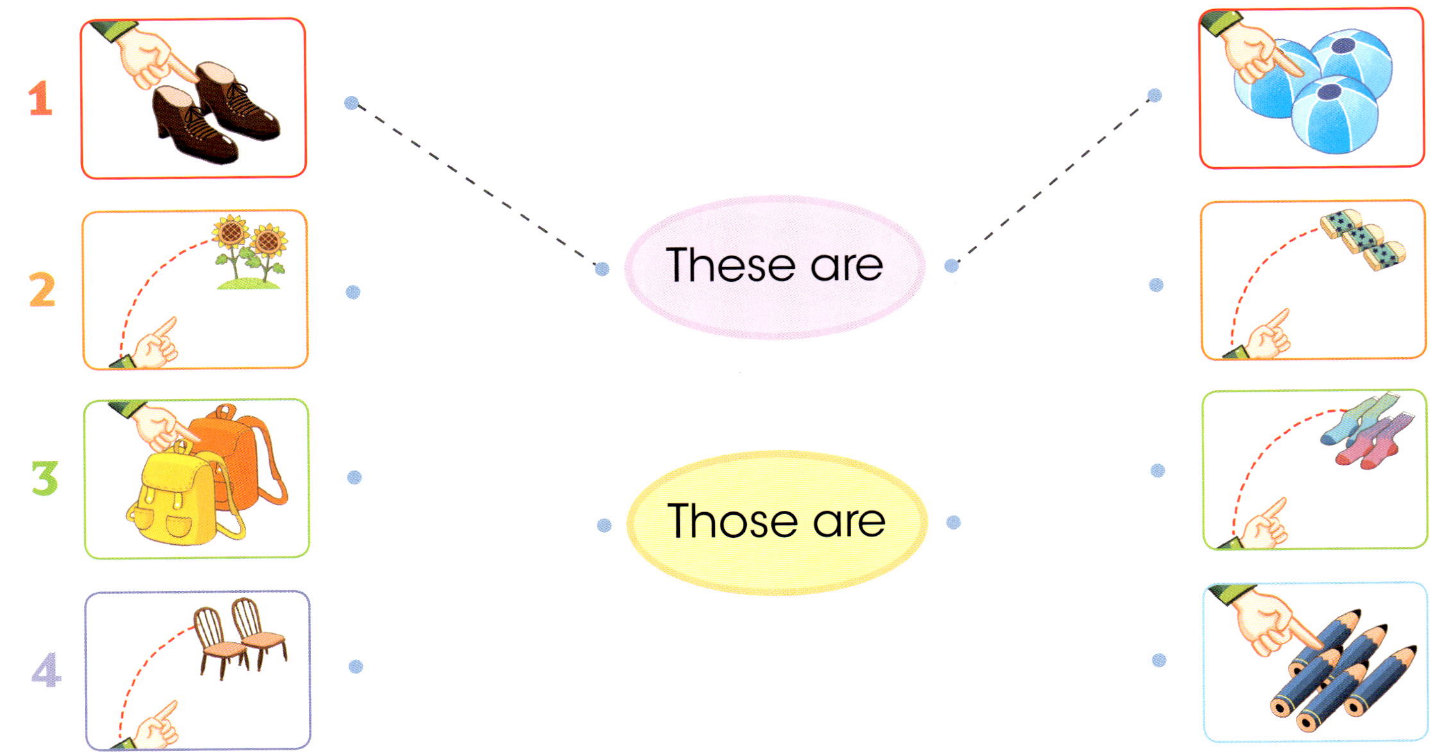

B. Fill in the blanks and circle the correct words.

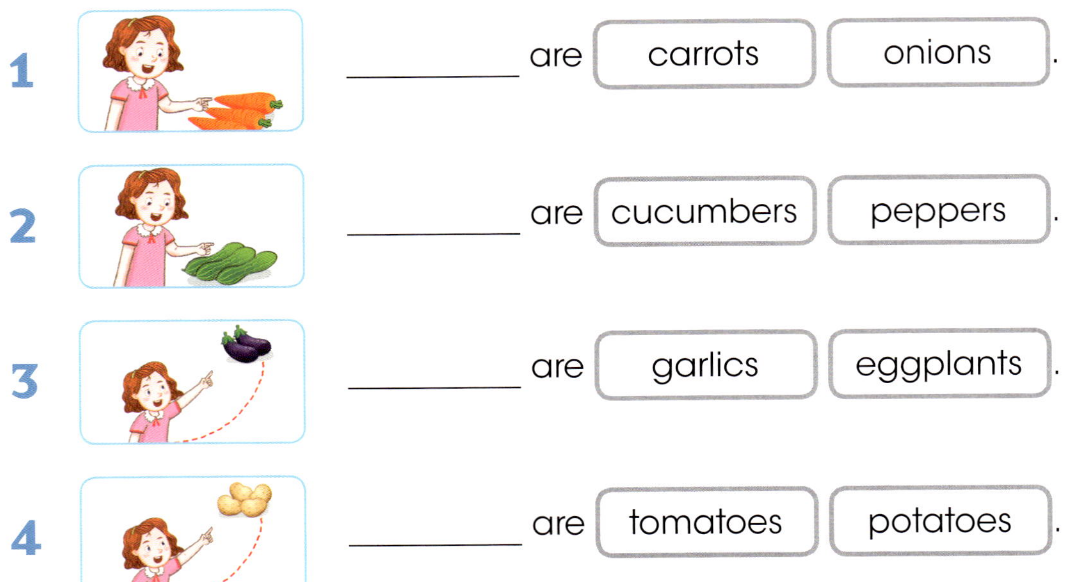

Put the pictures on any table.

Then say the sentences out loud.

For example: These are onions. / Those are onions.

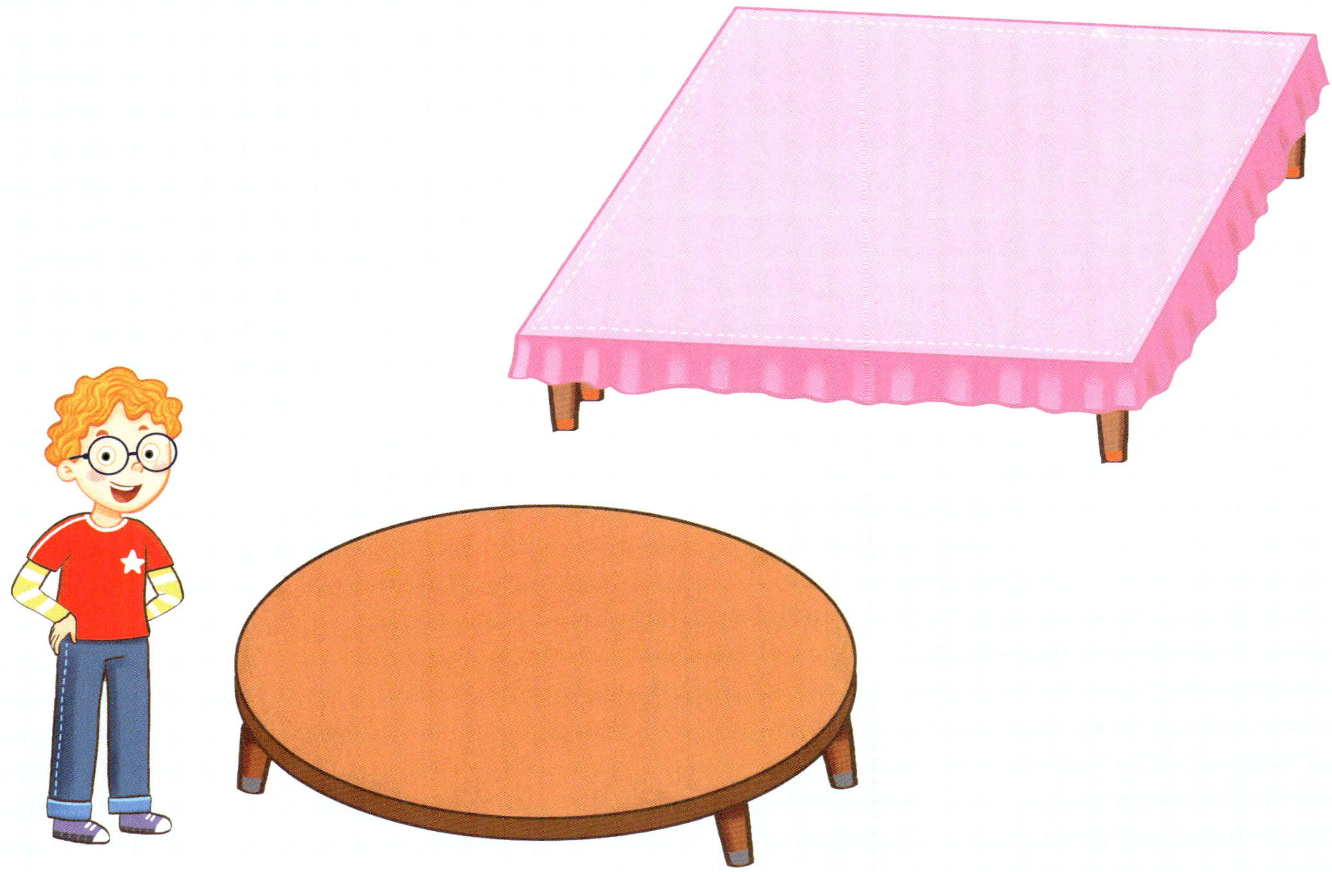

14

GRAM WRITING Correct the mistakes in red and rewrite the sentences.

1 This are tomatoes. I like them.

---

2 Look over there. These are carrots.

Unit 15 — It Is Spring

☐ **Listen** ☐ **Repeat** ☐ **Point**

sunny

spring

rainy

summer

windy

fall

snowy

winter

 **GRAM WORDS** Track 44  **ABC** **Listen and number the pictures in order.** Track 45

winter

spring

rainy

fall

snowy

summer

It Is + Season / Weather

It is + season / weather

	Season	Weather	
It is (=It's)	spring summer fall winter	sunny rainy windy snowy	.
It is			?

Examples

- It is spring.
- It is summer.
- It is sunny.
- It is rainy.
- Is it windy? – Yes, it is. / No, it isn't.

GRAM **CHECK UP**   Look and write O or X.

1 

It is spring.

2 

It is fall.

3 

It is snowy.

4 

It is rainy.

5 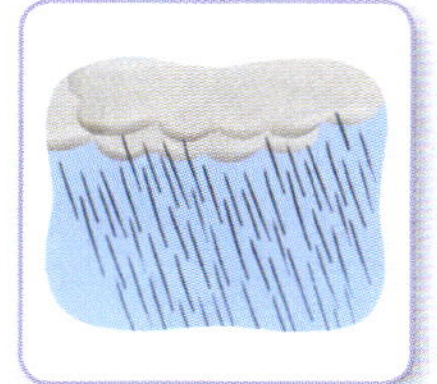

It is winter.

6 

It is sunny.

GRAM PRACTICE

A. Fill in the blanks like the example given.

It <u>is</u> winter.

1

It ________ ________.

2

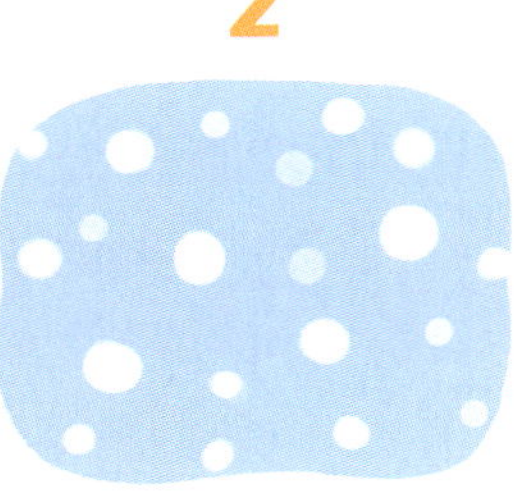

________ is snowy.

3

It is ________.

4

________ ________ spring.

5

It is ________.

B. Fill in the blanks like the example given.

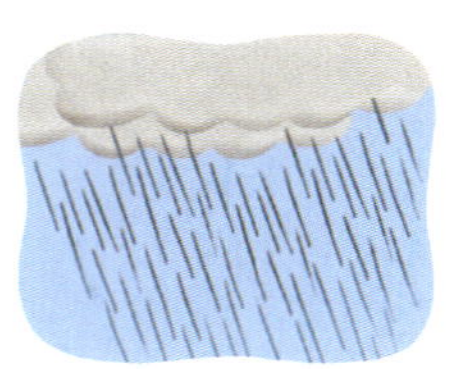

A: <u>Is</u> it rainy?
B: Yes, <u>it</u> <u>is</u>.

1

A: ________ ________ windy?
B: No, ________ ________.

2

A: ________ ________ fall?
B: No, ________ ________.

3

A: ________ ________ summer?
B: Yes, ________ ________.

4

A: ________ ________ winter?
B: Yes, ________ ________.

5

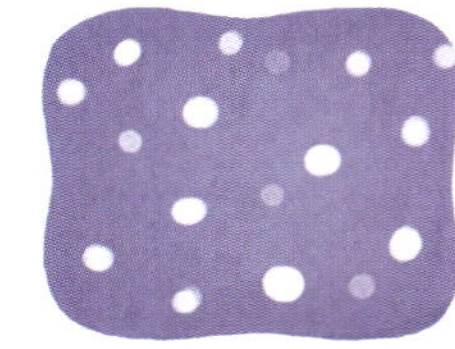

A: ________ ________ rainy?
B: No, ________ ________.

Season & Weather Spinner

Use a pencil and a paper clip. Spin the paper clip.

Then ask a question and answer it. (For example, *"It is spring."*)

GRAM WRITING — Correct the mistakes in red and rewrite the sentences.

1 It are winter. Is it snowy. I love winter.

2 it is spring. They is sunny. I love spring.

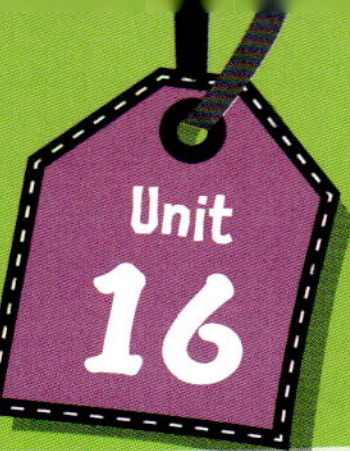

Unit 16 What Is That?

Track 46 ☐ Listen ☐ Repeat ☐ Point

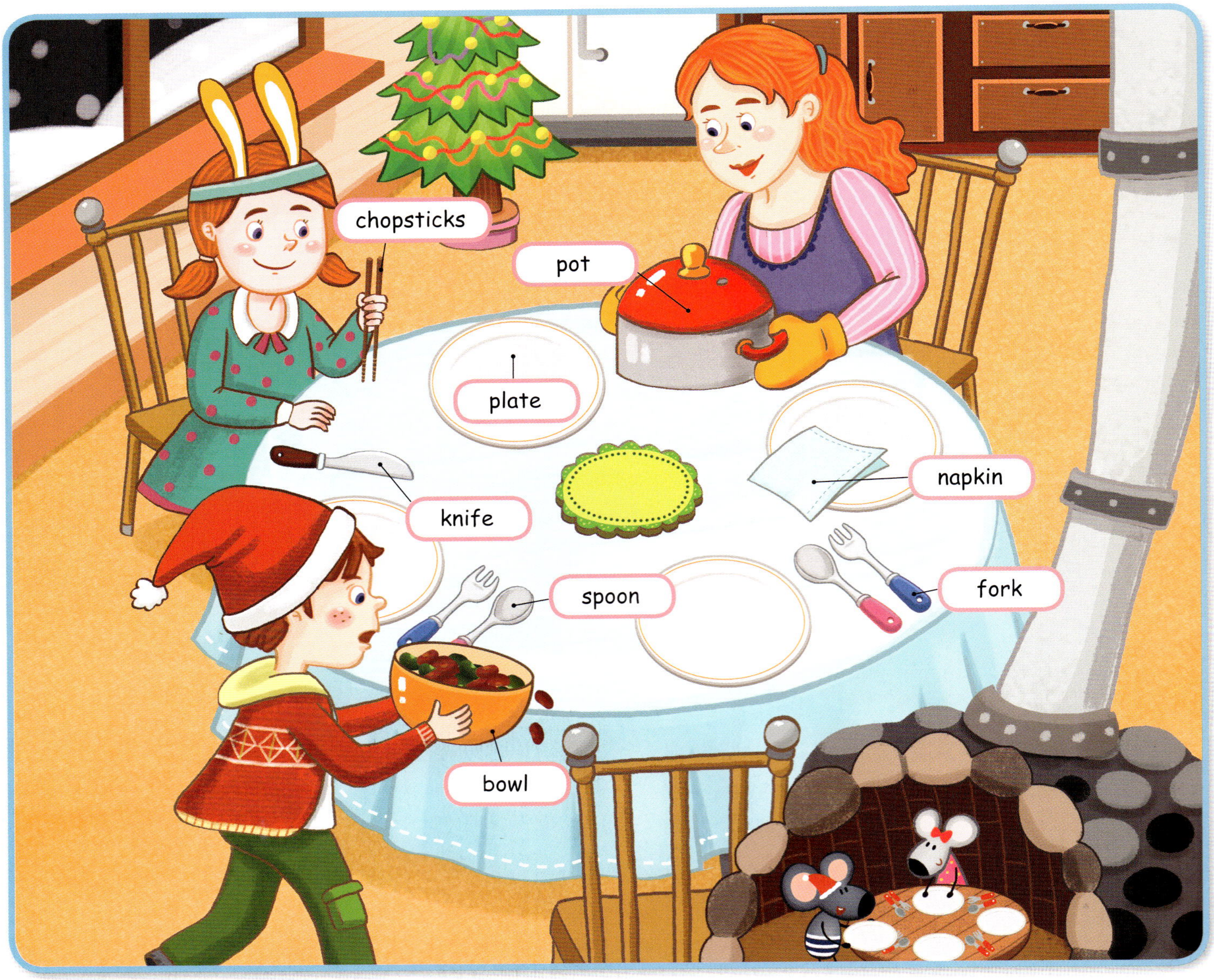

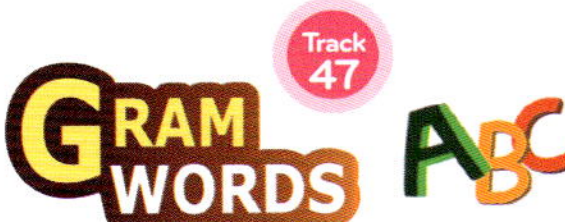

GRAM WORDS Track 47 ABC Listen and number the pictures in order. Track 48

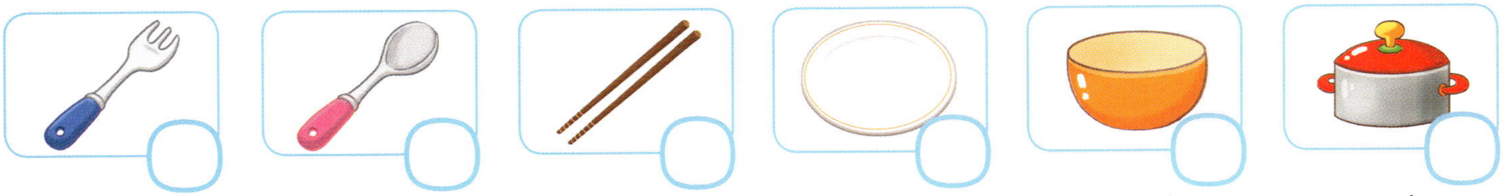

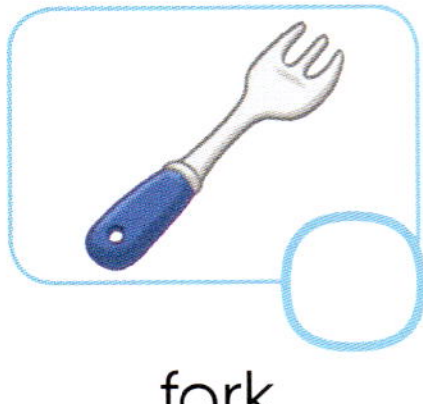

fork	spoon	chopsticks	plate	bowl	pot

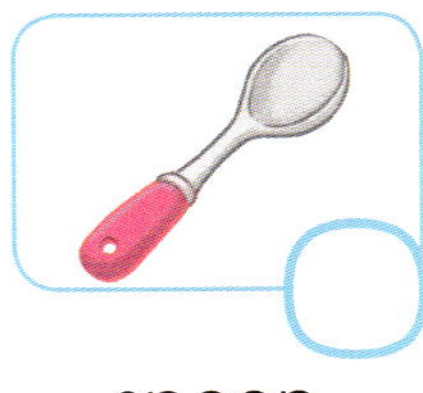

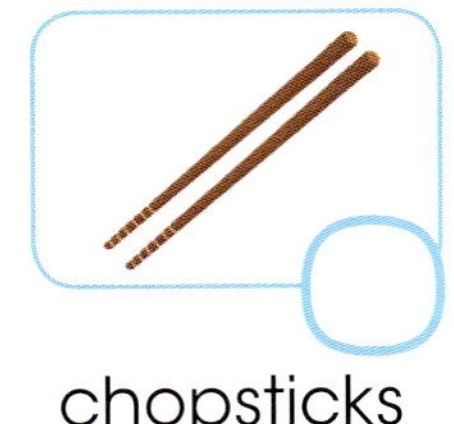

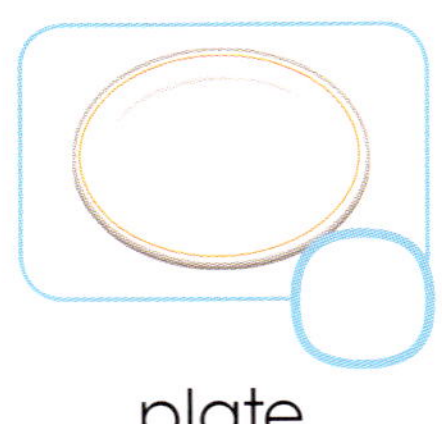

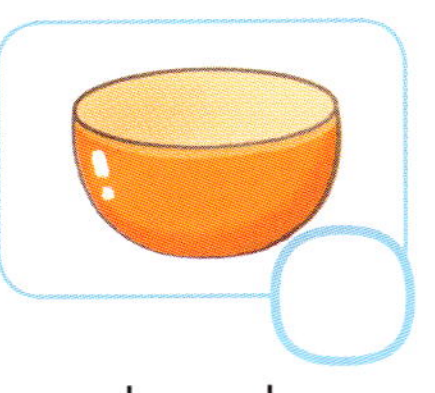

What Is This? / What Are Those?

What + Be verb ~ ?

Singular			Plural		
What	is	this?	What	are	these?
		that?			those?

- this/these : close to us
- that/those : far from us

Examples

- **What is this?** – It is (=It's) a spoon.   **What is that?** – It is (=It's) a fork.
- **What is these?** – They are (=They're) chopsticks.
- **What is those?** – They are (=They're) bowls.

GRAM CHECK UP   Look and write O or X.

1 

What is that?

2 

What is this?

3 

What are these?

4 

What is this?

5 

What are these?

6 

What is that?

16

GRAM PRACTICE

A. Look and write the words.

1 _______ is that?

2 What is _______ ?

3 _______ are these?

4 _______ are those?

5 What is _______ ?

6 _______ _______ those?

B. Fill in the blanks like the example given.

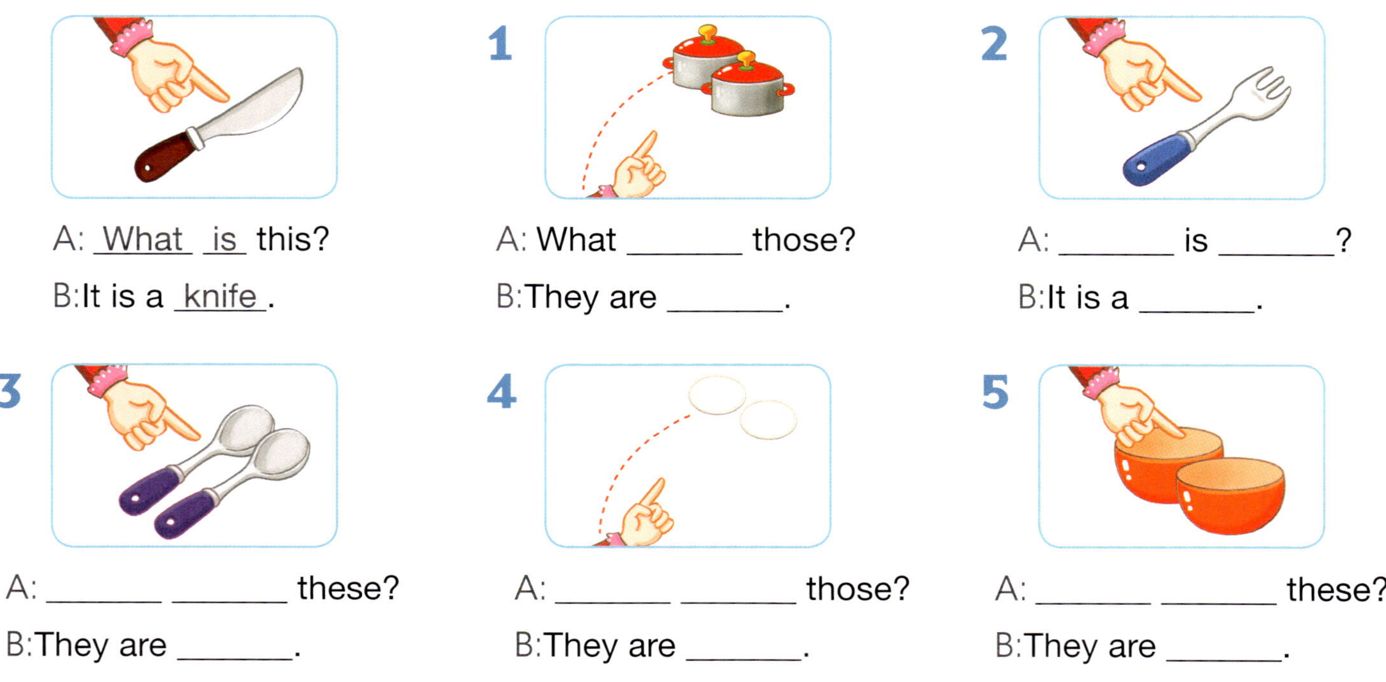

A: <u>What</u> <u>is</u> this?
B: It is a <u>knife</u>.

1
A: What _______ those?
B: They are _______.

2
A: _______ is _______?
B: It is a _______.

3
A: _______ _______ these?
B: They are _______.

4
A: _______ _______ those?
B: They are _______.

5
A: _______ _______ these?
B: They are _______.

Dice Game

Cut out the die and glue it together. Roll the die and ask questions like the example given. And answer the questions.

Correct the mistakes in red and rewrite the sentences.

1   What **are** this? It is a fork.

2   **Who** are those? **It** are spoons.

GRAM GRAM PLUS Book1

[Track 1] Page 8

Unit 01. Around Us

Listen and repeat the words. Then point to the pictures.
school
teacher
boy
girl
student
playground
park
dog
tree
bird

[Track 2]

[GRAM WORDS]
Listen and repeat.
student
teacher
school
park
dog
desk

[Track 03]

Listen and number the pictures in order.
1. park
2. desk
3. student
4. teacher
5. school
6. dog

[Track 04] Page 12

Unit 02. Things In The House

Listen and repeat the words. Then point to the pictures.
book
watch
umbrella
picture
door
table
chair
dish
cup
apple
fork
egg

[Track 05]

[GRAM WORDS]
Listen and repeat.
a cup
an apple
a dish
a watch
a book
an umbrella

[Track 06]

Listen and number the pictures in order.
1. an apple
2. a watch
3. an umbrella
4. a cup
5. a book
6. a dish

[Track 07] Page 16

Unit 03. My Family

Listen and repeat the words. Then point to the pictures.
grandfather
grandmother
mother
father
brother
sister
uncle
aunt
cousin
puppy

[Track 08]

[GRAM WORDS]
Listen and repeat.
grandfather
father
brother
grandmother
mother
sister

[Track 09]

Listen and number the pictures in order.
1. sister
2. mother
3. grandfather
4. brother
5. grandmother
6. father

[Track 10] Page 20

Unit 04. Happy Family

Listen and repeat the words. Then point to the pictures.
grandparents
wife
husband
parents
wife
husband

son

daughter

[GRAM WORDS]

Listen and repeat.

grandparents

son

daughter

wife

parents

husband

[Track 12]

Listen and number the pictures in order.

1. husband
2. parents
3. grandparents
4. son
5. wife
6. daughter

[Track 13] Page 24

Unit 05. Neighbors

Listen and repeat the words. Then point to the pictures.

baker

driver

painter

police officer

firefighter

street cleaner

nurse

hair dresser

[Track 14]

[GRAM WORDS]

Listen and repeat.

baker

driver

painter

police officer

nurse

firefighter

[Track 15]

Listen and number the pictures in order.

1. firefighter
2. nurse
3. painter
4. baker
5. driver
6. police officer

[Track 16] Page 28

Unit 06. Jobs

Listen and repeat the words. Then point to the pictures.

doctor

designer

singer

scientist

pilot

farmer

cook

dancer

[Track 17]

[GRAM WORDS]

Listen and repeat.

doctor

singer

cook

farmer

pilot

designer

[Track 18]

Listen and number the pictures in order.

1. pilot
2. cook
3. farmer
4. doctor
5. singer
6. designer

[Track 19] Page 32

Unit 07. Our Classroom

Listen and repeat the words. Then point to the pictures.

blackboard

teacher

classmate

class president

desk

scissors

glue

locker

computer

[Track 20]

[GRAM WORDS]

Listen and repeat.

locker

computer

blackboard

desk

classmate

class president

[Track 21]

Listen and number the pictures in order.

1. desk
2. blackboard
3. computer

4. locker
5. class president
6. classmate

[Track 22] Page 36

Unit 08. Favorite Subjects

Listen and repeat the words. Then point to the pictures.

math
English
art
social studies
P.E. (Physical Education)
history
science
music

[Track 23]

[GRAM WORDS]
Listen and repeat.

math
English
art
history
science
music

[Track 24]

Listen and number the pictures in order.

1. music
2. science
3. English
4. math
5. history
6. art

[Track 25] Page 40

Unit 09. I Am Tall

Listen and repeat the words. Then point to the pictures.

tall
short
fat
thin
pretty
ugly
young
old
strong
weak

[Track 26]

[GRAM WORDS]
Listen and repeat.

fat
thin
pretty
short
tall
ugly

[Track 27]

Listen and number the pictures in order.

1. fat
2. tall
3. ugly
4. pretty
5. thin
6. short

[Track 28] Page 44

Unit 10. Jake Is Angry

Listen and repeat the words. Then point to the pictures.

happy
sad
jealous
surprised
excited
angry
full
hungry

[Track 29]

[GRAM WORDS]
Listen and repeat.

happy
surprised
sad
angry
excited
jealous

[Track 30]

Listen and number the pictures in order.

1. jealous
2. angry
3. excited
4. sad
5. happy
6. surprised

[Track 31] Page 48

Unit 11. It Is Red Balloon

Listen and repeat the words. Then point to the pictures.

red
orange
yellow
green
white
blue
big
small
long
short

[Track 32]

[GRAM WORDS]
Listen and repeat.

yellow

green

blue

red

long

small

[Track 33]

Listen and number the pictures in order.

1. blue
2. red
3. long
4. small
5. green
6. yellow

[Track 34] Page 52

Unit 12. This Is My Hat

Listen and repeat the words. Then point to the pictures.

sweater

blouse

skirt

pants

shoes

socks

jeans

jacket

hat

coat

[Track 35]

[GRAM WORDS]

Listen and repeat.

pants

jacket

blouse

skirt

coat

sweater

[Track 36]

Listen and number the pictures in order.

1. blouse
2. coat
3. sweater
4. skirt
5. jacket
6. pants

[Track 37] Page 56

Unit 13. This Is A Pear

Listen and repeat the words. Then point to the pictures.

pear

grapes

strawberry

banana

watermelon

cherry

kiwi

[Track 38]

[GRAM WORDS]

Listen and repeat.

strawberry

cherry

kiwi

watermelon

grapes

pear

[Track 39]

Listen and number the pictures in order.

1. pear
2. cherry
3. strawberry
4. grapes
5. kiwi
6. watermelon

[Track 40] Page 60

Unit 14. Those Are Onions

Listen and repeat the words. Then point to the pictures.

onion

tomato

potato

cucumber

carrot

pepper

garlic

eggplant

[Track 41]

[GRAM WORDS]

Listen and repeat.

onion

tomato

potato

eggplant

cucumber

carrot x2

[Track 42]

Listen and number the pictures in order.

1. carrot
2. cucumber
3. eggplant
4. potato
5. tomato
6. onion

[Track 43] Page 64

Unit 15. It Is Spring

Listen and repeat the words. Then point to the pictures.

spring

summer

fall

winter

sunny

rainy

windy

snowy

[Track 44]

[GRAM WORDS]

Listen and repeat.

winter

spring

rainy

fall

snowy

summer

[Track 45]

Listen and number the pictures in order.

1. summer
2. snowy
3. fall
4. spring
5. winter
6. rainy

[Track 46] Page 68

Unit 16. What Is That?

Listen and repeat the words. Then point to the pictures.

bowl

plate

fork

spoon

knife

chopsticks

napkin

pot

[Track 47]

Listen and repeat.

fork

spoon

chopsticks

plate

bowl

pot

[Track 48]

Listen and number the pictures in order.

1. pot
2. bowl
3. plate
4. chopsticks
5. fork
6. spoon

Answers

Unit 01. Around Us

[GRAM WORDS] p.8

3-4-5-1-6-2

[GRAM CHECK UP] p.9

1. PE
2. PL
3. A
4. A
5. PL
6. T

[GRAM PRACTICE] p.10

A.

1. People  

2. Things 

3. Places 

4. Animals  

B.

1. desk　park　dog　boy

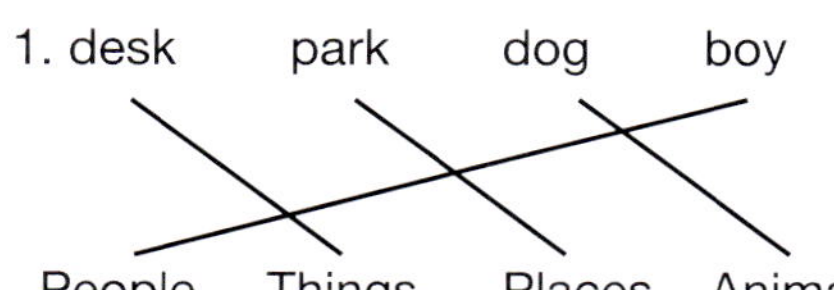

People　Things　Places　Animals

[FUNNY GRAM] p.11

People: teacher
Things: desk
Animals: bird

[GRAM WRITING] p.11

1. My favorite **thing** is my robot.
2. My favorite **animal** is the frog.

Unit 02. Things In The House

[GRAM WORDS] p.12

4-1-6-2-5-3

[GRAM CHECK UP] p.13

1. X
2. O
3. O
4. O
5. X
6. O

[GRAM PRACTICE] p.14

A.

1. **a** book
2. **an** umbrella
3. **a** cup
4. dish**es**
5. watch**es**
6. apple**s**
7. **an** egg
8. picture**s**
9. **a** chair

B.

1. three **books**
2. five **apples**
3. an **umbrella**
4. seven **eggs**
5. three **dishes**

[FUNNY GRAM] p.15

a watch → watches
an apple → apples
a book → books
a dish → dishes

a picture → pictures
a door → doors
a fork → forks
an umbrella → umbrellas
an egg → eggs
a table → tables
a cup → cups

[GRAM WRITING] p.15

1. I have ten **eggs**. I eat two **eggs**.
2. I eat five **apples**. Oh, I'm full.

Unit 03. My Family

[GRAM WORDS] p.16

3-6-4-5-2-1

[GRAM CHECK UP] p.17

1. O
2. O
3. X
4. X
5. X
6. O

[GRAM PRACTICE] p.18

A.

1. She
2. He
3. It

B.

1. father → **He**
2. mother → **She**
3. brother → **He**
4. sister → **She**
5. me → **I**
6. puppy → **It**

[FUNNY GRAM] p.19

She → He → I → You → It

[GRAM WRITING] p.19

1. **She** is my mother. **I** love my mother.
2. **He** is my grandfather. **He** is generous.

Unit 04. Happy Family

[GRAM WORDS] p.20

3-4-6-5-2-1

[GRAM CHECK UP] p.21

1. X
2. O
3. O
4. X
5. O
6. O

[GRAM PRACTICE] p.22

A.

1. We
2. You
3. They
4. We

B.

1. We
2. They
3. We
4. They
5. They

[GRAM WRITING] p.23

1. I have two sisters. **They** are kind.
2. My parents are generous. **They** love me.

Unit 05. Neighbors

[GRAM WORDS] p.24

4-5-3-6-2-1

[GRAM CHECK UP] p.25

1. X (We are)
2. O
3. O
4. O
5. X (She is)
6. X (They are)

[GRAM PRACTICE] p.26

A.

1. He – is – He's
2. She – is – She's
3. I – am – I'm
4. You – are – You're
5. They – are – They're
6. We – are – We're

B.

1. He is a **baker**.
2. **She** is a **hair dresser**.
3. They **are firefighters**.
4. She **is** a **nurse**.
5. **He** is a **painter**.

[GRAM WRITING] p.27

1. She **is** a baker. She bakes fresh bread.
2. He **is** a firefighter. She is a nurse. They **are** our neighbors.

Unit 06. Jobs

[GRAM WORDS] p.28

4-5-2-3-1-6

[GRAM CHECK UP] p.29

1. X / **We aren't** doctors.
2. O
3. X / **They aren't** dancers.
4. O
5. X / **She isn't** a designer.
6. X / **You aren't** a farmer.

[GRAM PRACTICE] p.30

A.

1. I – am not – I'm not
2. She – is not – She isn't
3. He – is not – He isn't
4. You – are not – You aren't
5. They – are not – They aren't
6. We – are not – We aren't

B.

1. She is **not** a pilot. She is a **cook**.
2. I **am** not a **singer**. I am a **dancer**.
3. They **aren't (are not)** farmers. They are **doctors**.
4. He is **not** a designer. He is a **pilot**.
5. We **aren't (are not)** cooks. We are **farmers**.

[GRAM WRITING] p.31

1. I **am not (I'm not)** a student. I **am** a teacher.
2. He **isn't** a pilot. He is a designer.

Unit 07. Our Classroom

[GRAM WORDS] p.32

4-3-2-1-6-5

[GRAM CHECK UP] p.33

1. Are
2. Are
3. Is
4. Is
5. Are
6. Is

[GRAM PRACTICE] p.34

A.

1. Yes, it is.
2. Yes, they are.
3. Yes, I am.
4. No, they aren't.

B.

1. Are

2. Is

3. he

4. they

5. Are

6. Are

7. Is

8. Are

9. it

10. Are

[GRAM WRITING] p.35

1. A: **Is** he the class president?

   B: Yes, he **is**. He is nice.

2. I am a teacher. **Are** you a student?

Unit 08. Favorite Subjects

[GRAM WORDS] p.36

4-3-6-5-2-1

[GRAM CHECK UP] p.37

1. Who

2. Who

3. What

4. Who

5. Who

6. What

[GRAM PRACTICE] p.38

A.

1. Who

2. Who, He

3. What

4. What, They

B.

1. Who are they?

2. Who is he?

3. Who are we?

4. What is it?

5. What are they?

6. Who are you?

[GRAM WRITING] p. 39

1.

A: **Who** is she?

B: **She** is my art teacher. I like her.

2.

A: What **are** they?

B: **They** are pens and pencils.

Unit 09. I Am Tall

[GRAM WORDS] p.40

1-5-4-6-2-3

[GRAM CHECK UP] p.41

1. tall

2. young

3. thin

4. strong

5. ugly

[GRAM PRACTICE] p.42

A.

1. f**at** – t**hin**

2. stro**ng** – **wea**k

3. t**all** – sh**ort**

4. p**re**tty - u**gl**y

B.

1. thin

2. young

3. pretty

4. old

5. ugly

6. short

7. strong

8. tall

[GRAM WRITING] p. 43

1. Steve is not **thin**. He **is** fat.

2. Jenny **is** short and Amy is **tall**.

Unit 10. Jake Is Angry

[GRAM WORDS] p.44

5-6-4-2-3-1

[GRAM CHECK UP] p.45

1. happy

2. sad

3. surprised

4. hungry

5. angry

6. jealous

[GRAM PRACTICE] p.46

A.

1. hungry

2. angry

3. happy

4. excited

5. jealous

6. surprised

7. full

8. sad

B.

1. She is happy.

2. I am full.

3. I am hungry.

4. They are excited.

5. You are angry.

6. He is surprised.

[GRAM WRITING] p.47

1. **Are** you happy? – Yes, I **am** happy.

2. Are they **hungry**? – No, **they** are full.

Unit 11. It Is A Red Balloon

[GRAM WORDS] p.48

6-5-1-2-3-4

[GRAM CHECK UP] p.49

1. red balloon

2. lcng snake

3. yellow pants

4. big tiger

5. orange bag

6. small flower

[GRAM PRACTICE] p.50

A.

1. It is a **big pig**.
2. The **balloon** is **yellow**.
3. It is a **long pencil**.
4. It is a **red flower**.
5. The bag is **small**.
 = It is a small **bag**.

B.

1. The pencil is long.
2. The cup is small.
3. The skirt is red.
4. The bag is white.
5. The lion is big.
6. The hat is green.

[GRAM WRITING] p.51

1. It is a **yellow flower**. It is beautiful.
2. The elephant **is big**. It is very big.

Unit 12. This Is My Hat

[GRAM WORDS] p.52

6-5-1-4-2-3

[GRAM CHECK UP] p.53

1. X (his jeans)
2. O
3. O
4. O
5. X (his shoes)
6. O

[GRAM PRACTICE] p.54

A.

1. he – his
2. you – your
3. she – her
4. they – their
5. it – its
6. we – our
7. I – my
8. Jane – Jane's

B.

1. This is **my** jacket.
2. This is **her** skirt.
3. This is **your** blouse.
4. This is **our** classroom.

[GRAM WRITING] p.55

1. This is **my** jacket. I love it.
2. Is this **your** coat? It looks nice.

Unit 13. This Is A Pear

[GRAM WORDS] p.56

3-2-5-6-4-1

[GRAM CHECK UP] p.57

1. O
2. X (Those are)
3. O
4. X (That is)
5. X (This is)
6. O

[GRAM PRACTICE] p.58

A.

1.  This is – 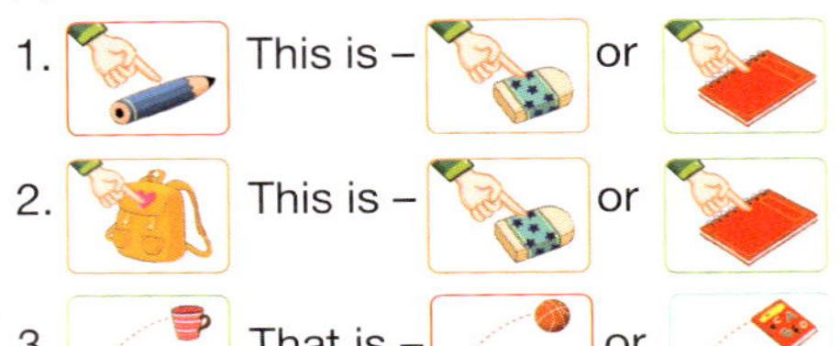 or

2. This is –

3. That is –

4. That is –

B.

1. **This** is an **orange**.
2. **That** is a **kiwi**.
3. **That** is a **pear**.
4. **This** is a **banana**.

[GRAM WRITING] p.59

1. This **is** a kiwi. I love kiwis.
2. Look over there. **That** is a tree.

Unit 14. Those Are Onions

[GRAM WORDS] p.60

6-5-4-3-2-1

[GRAM CHECK UP] p.61

1. O
2. O
3. X (Those are)
4. O
5. X (These are)
6. X (These are)

[GRAM PRACTICE] p.62

A.

1. 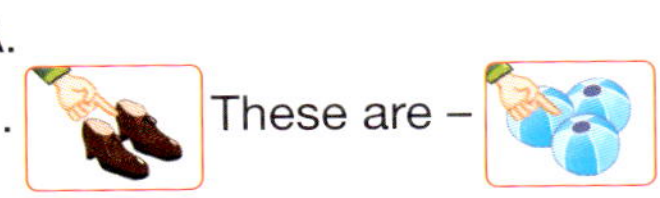 These are – or

2. 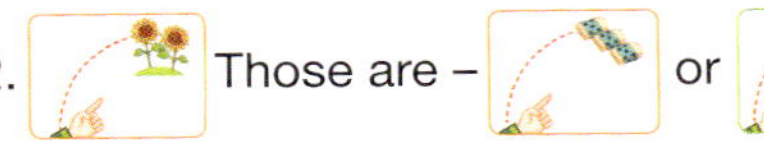 Those are – or

3.  These are – or

4. 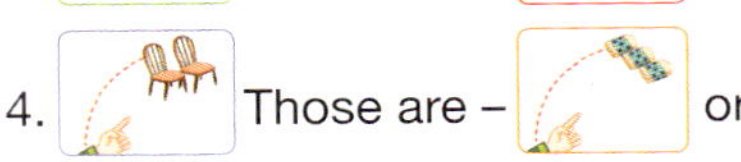 Those are –  or

B.

1. **These** are **carrots**.
2. **These** are **cucumbers**.
3. **Those** are **eggplants**.
4. **Those** are **potatoes**.

[GRAM WRITING] p.63

1. **These** are tomatoes. I like them.
2. Look over there. **Those** are carrots.

Unit 15. It Is Spring

[GRAM WORDS] p.64

5-4-6-3-2-1

[GRAM CHECK UP] p.65

1. O
2. X (It is summer.)
3. X (It is windy.)
4. O
5. O
6. O

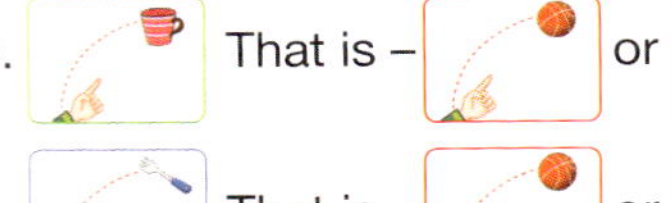

[GRAM PRACTICE] p.66

A.

1. It **is fall**.

2. **It** is snowy.

3. It is **rainy**.

4. **It is** spring.

5. It is **windy**.

B.

1. **Is it** windy? – No, **it isn't**.

2. **Is it** fall? – No, **it isn't**.

3. **Is it** summer? – Yes, **it is**.

4. **Is it** winter? – Yes, **it is**.

5. **Is it** rainy? – No, **it isn't**.

[GRAM WRITING] p.67

1. It **is** winter. **It is** snowy. I love winter.

2. **It** is spring. **It** is sunny. I love spring.

Unit 16 What Is That?

[GRAM WORDS] p.68

5-6-4-3-2-1

[GRAM CHECK UP] p.69

1. X (What are those?)

2. X (What are these?)

3. X (What are those?)

4. O

5. X (What is this?)

6. O

[GRAM PRACTICE] p.70

A.

1. **What** is that?

2. What is **this**?

3. **What** are these?

4. **What** are those?

5. What is **this**?

6. **What are** those?

B.

1. What **are** those?

   They are **pots**.

2. **What** is **this**?

   It is a **fork**.

3. **What are** these?

   They are **spoons**.

4. **What are** those?

   They are **plates**.

5. **What are** these?

   They are **bowls**.

[GRAM WRITING] p.71

1. What **is** this? It is a fork.

2. **What** are those? **They** are spoons.

GramGram Plus 1

First Printing 2013.10.25

Author Hyunjeong, Kim

Consultant Prof. Eunyoung, Park

Editorial Supervisor LLS English Research Center

Publisher Kiseon, Lee

Publishing Company JPLUS

62, World Cup-ro 31-gil, Mapo-gu, Seoul, Korea

Telephone 02-332-8320

Fax 02-332-8321

Homepage www.jplus114.com

Registration Number 10-1680

Registration Date 1998.12.09

ISBN 979-11-5601-001-2(64740)

memo

Unit 12 Bingo Game p.55
his
her our my your
their
Unit 14 Vegetable Tables p.63
onions
tomatoes
potatoes
cucumbers
carrots
peppers
garlic
eggplants

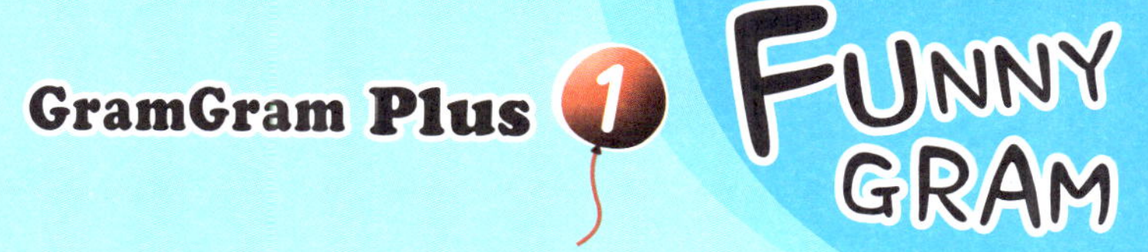

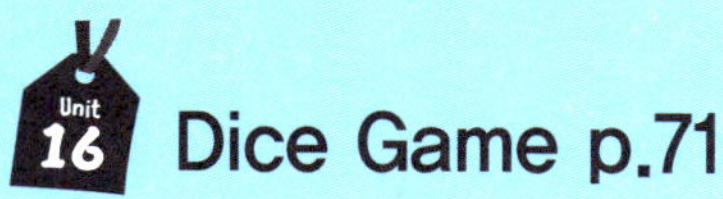

Dice Game p.71

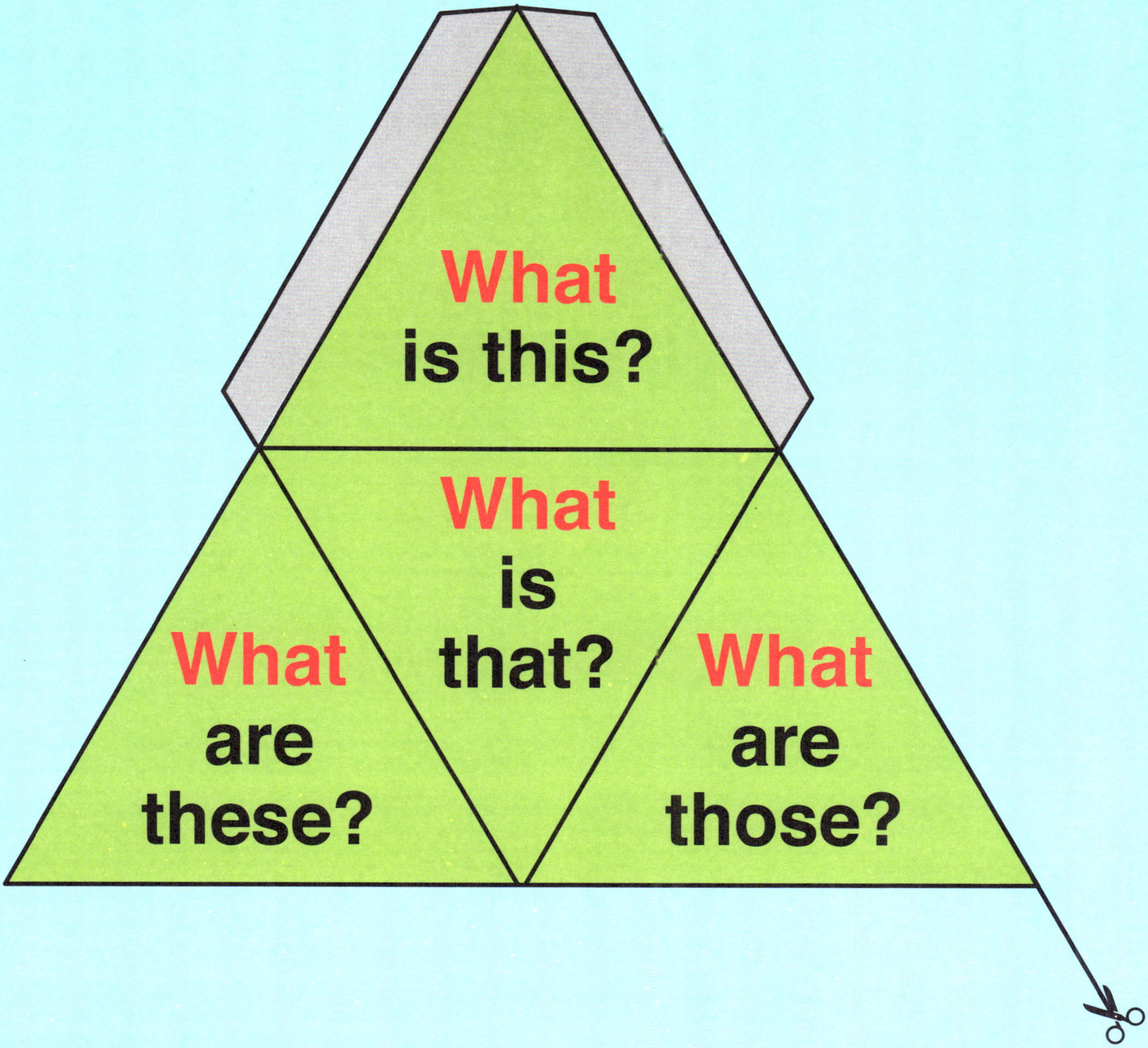